OLD UNIVERSITY BOAT HOUSE ON NORTH BANK OF CHARLES RIVER

The crew in foreground is the '85 University Crew, with Keyes, '87 at No. 3 in place of Burgess, and J. S. Russell, '87, a substitute, at Bow

Twenty Harvard Crews

BY

GEORGE SALTONSTALL MUMFORD

OF HARVARD, CLASS OF 1887

WITH ILLUSTRATIONS

CAMBRIDGE

HARVARD UNIVERSITY PRESS

LONDON : HUMPHREY MILFORD

OXFORD UNIVERSITY PRESS

1923

PRINTED AT THE HARVARD UNIVERSITY PRESS
CAMBRIDGE, MASS., U.S.A.

FOREWORD

THESE twenty years proved a formative period in Harvard's athletic history. It was during this time that football developed from a rough-and-tumble contest into a real test of skill in organizing formations and effective combinations of men for both attack and defense.

In rowing the period began with the University crew under the complete control of the captain, with an advisory committee of graduates of his own choosing, and after a series of alternations consisting of graduate control, control by a coach, with intervening years of control again by the captain, it ended just where it began, with the captain and an advisory rowing committee selected by him.

When this period began, eight-oared rowing in this country had been going on for only six years, while in England it had been practised for half a century. The sliding seat had been in use only ten years.

Perhaps the most marked characteristic at that time in rowing conditions, especially at Harvard, was the attitude of suspicion on the part of amateur college oarsmen toward the professional sculler and oarsman, his methods, his style and record. This seems especially surprising now in view of the recognized fact that professional sculling, as exemplified in the performances of Edward Hanlon, of Toronto, as well as of Beach the Australian who defeated the former for the world's championship, attained before 1880 the highest standard that it has ever reached. It is safe to say that Hanlon was the most perfect sculler and boatman that ever sat in a shell. The lessons that college oarsmen might have learned from watching and copying him were allowed to work through all too slowly to reach them.

"Good form" in rowing had become a definitely accepted style with the English College and University crews, but the conception of it and its application by various coaches of American college crews had led to such great varieties and divergences in actual practice as to leave the original model scarcely recognizable anywhere in American amateur rowing. This does not mean that some of our eights did not in fact previous to this time employ the style known as "good form." The Harvard University crews of 1878 and 1879 were notable examples of such rowing, but in general it did not appear to be understood by coaches of college crews.

BOSTON, November, 1922.

CONTENTS

[v]

LIST OF ILLUSTRATIONS

TWENTY HARVARD CREWS

1882

Harvard won by fifty feet

The University boat house was located on the left or north bank of the Charles River, not very far below where the Weld boat house now stands.

The river was a tideway, quite narrow at low water and quite roomy at high. The rush of the tide frequently made the bridges very difficult for the coxswains to negotiate, and broken oars, especially in the eight-oared shells, were by no means unusual. The only measured four miles for practice were from the site of the present Weld boat house through and around the right-hand edge of the basin to Craigie's bridge where now stands the Charles River dam. The Harvard bridge carrying Massachusetts Avenue from the Back Bay of Boston into Central Square, Cambridge, was not built until 1888. Racing was, of course, impossible anywhere on the river except through the Back Bay basin below the Longwood bridge.

In June, 1881, spectators standing inside the old wall bordering the Charles River in the alley-way behind the Beacon Street houses, on a windy afternoon, watched two eight-oared crews racing down the $1\frac{7}{8}$ miles course. Near the finish it was evident that the leading crew had the race well in hand, and the three or four lengths that separated the boats when the first of them reached the finish line was a fair measure of its superiority in power and form. This race was the annual contest of the Harvard and Columbia Freshman crews, and for fifteen years it furnished the only real try-out which provided Varsity material for future Harvard crews.

[3]

The '84 Freshman crew that won on this day furnished its quota to the Varsity crews for the next two or three years, just as the '83 Freshman crew had done a year previously. In those days for some reason it was looked upon as a stroke of wisdom on the part of Harvard not to encourage in the minds of Yale men the idea that intercollegiate Freshman contests were either desirable or proper. Hence, Harvard Freshmen rowed Columbia Freshmen, and Yale Freshmen had no race.

Charles Mifflin Hammond '83, of New London, Connecticut, who rowed in the 1881 Harvard University crew, which was beaten by Yale by a couple of boat lengths, was elected captain of the 1882 University crew.

The rowing season in preparation for the '82 race began with all but two of the members of the '81 crew still in College and some excellent material from the '84 Freshman crew.

This season especially marked a period lasting for perhaps three or four years, during which boat builders and professional oarsmen experimented with racing shells and with college crews over various mechanical devices for increasing the speed. New oarlocks were invented, new forms of seats sliding on rollers, oars with strange-looking blades, notably the so-called "leg-o'-mutton" oars, which were shaped somewhat like attenuated boat rudders with long handles. Some of these devices were accepted as decided improvements, and the sliding seats and the oarlocks of that time are identical with those still in use; in fact, since then there have been practically no improvements in mechanical rowing devices. As was to be expected, some of the experiments proved to be failures.

Michael F. Davis, a well-known professional oarsman and boat rigger, was employed by the Yale University crew of this year to rig their boat and to advise them in coaching matters. This apparently was contrary to the wishes and advice of Robert J. Cook, Yale '76, who before this and long after held a high position of authority in Yale rowing. The Yale crew was regarded as of unusually fine material, the candidates being almost uniformly of splendid physique, and of size well above the average college oarsman. Mr. Davis persuaded Louis K. Hull '83, the Yale captain, apparently with the full approval of the rest of the crew, to adopt a form of stroke known in those days as the professional stroke, although many of the best professional scullers appeared to repudiate it in many of its details. The principle apparently was to have the men row as many strokes to the minute as possible without shortening, and necessarily with a disregard of the English theory of due control of the recover. Also during the last month of their training they proposed to row over the course as many times as possible with a view to attaining complete uniformity of style. If this Yale crew could get perfectly together with a stroke ranging from 45 to 50 strokes to the minute, with their extraordinary physical advantages, it was thought that they could beat any possible competitor.

Davis conceived the idea that if the boat was divided up, by spacing, into four pair-oars, the men would be able to row more effectively; accordingly, between No. 2 and No. 3, No. 4 and No. 5, and No. 6 and No. 7, the boat was lengthened out for a couple of extra feet, making the shell nearly 70 feet long instead of 59 feet, the usual length. The crew was also equipped with the "leg-o'-mutton" oars. The newspapers gave a great deal of attention to the experiments that were being made with this Yale crew, and for some reason or other, it became looked upon popularly as representing an American stroke and a real American spirit as opposed to a Harvard–English stroke and Harvard "indifference," which latter represented doubtless in the eyes of the newspaper public the spirit of the "effete European monarchies."

The Harvard crew was coached by Mr. William A. Bancroft '78, and Mr. R. C. Watson '69 was in constant consultation with Captain Hammond, and his advice and assistance was considered of no little importance in the work of the crew.

Harvard was scheduled to row the Columbia University eight one week previous to the Yale race. The Harvard crew reached New London about June 18th and settled in the new quarters located on the east side of the river five miles above the city of New London. This building had been erected the year before and paid for by money obtained chiefly through the generosity of a few loyal Harvard supporters and certain friends of Mr. Watson. The building still stands and is now used by the Harvard Freshmen.

It was the custom for Harvard to row Columbia first and Yale a week later, both races over the same course.

Shortly after the arrival of the Columbia crew at New London, their coxswain lost his life by drowning, and at the request of the Columbia rowing authorities, the Harvard–Columbia race was postponed for nine days, to be rowed at noon on the Monday following the Harvard–Yale race. After the Harvard–Yale race had been rowed, a demand was made by Columbia that the hour fixed for the Columbia race be changed. This demand and the attitude which Columbia's representatives took in the discussion

HARVARD QUARTERS: "RED TOP" IN 1884

From a photograph taken by Dr. J. N. Borland, of New London, Connecticut

that followed were held to be unreasonable by the Harvard men, and as they felt that with the conclusion of the Yale race the real aim and object of their year's work had been attained, and that no good end would be served by waiting further on Columbia's pleasure, the members of the Harvard crew on Sunday, two days after the Yale race, having as they supposed agreed with Columbia to call off the race, dispersed themselves to their several homes. Mr. Watson, the referee, having no knowledge of any agreement to call the race off, evidently supposed that it was left to him to award the race to Harvard or Columbia, as he might see fit and he eventually rendered a decision favorable to Columbia University, which the members of the Harvard crew apparently regarded as but an empty honor for their rivals.

After the Harvard crew had been in New London for a few days, Edward T. Cabot '83, who had rowed bow all through the season, was taken sick. It then appeared that no suitably trained substitute had accompanied the crew; that the eight men had been trained with great care for their several positions, but there was no one to take the place of any of the regular men at all their equal in rowing form, or who had received any sort of efficient coaching.

William W. Mumford '84 and H. R. Woodward '84 were respectively starboard and port substitutes, and had been rowing together in a pair-oar for a month or two without getting any attention to speak of from either captain or coach. They had both rowed in the '84 Freshman crew the previous June in the race against the Columbia Freshman crew. Mumford was placed in the eight at bow in place of Cabot. The change was a very serious matter for the crew, for, although he was a powerful man, his rowing form was crude, and during the few days' practice that he had previous to the race, he was unable to fall into the beat with the other seven men with perfect success.

A difficulty now arose owing to the difference in length between the Harvard and Yale shells. If the two boats started with their sterns even and finished by the bows, the Yale boat had an advantage of several feet over the four-mile course, which Harvard would have to overcome in order to have her bow finish even with the bow of the Yale boat. The dispute was finally compromised by deciding that they should finish by the sterns, a decision that was reached only after the two boats had arrived at the starting line.

Previous to the day of the race, the Yale crew, true to form, had been sent over the four-mile course an astonishing number of times. It apparently was no unusual feat for these men to row four miles down in the morning at 45 strokes to the minute or thereabouts, and row hard all the time, and then turn about and row home again at perhaps a little slower stroke, and repeat the performance that same afternoon, and do this day after day. Good form and the control of the slides seemed to be of minor importance. Good watermanship and many strokes to the minute were the essentials, and the long boat, with the curious seating of the men in pairs, gave this crew a decidedly unique appearance.

The race was rowed down stream at twenty minutes after eleven o'clock in the morning, Harvard having the west course and Yale the east, or Groton side. The Yale crew started off at 45 strokes to the minute, and the Harvard crew at about 38 strokes. The race was rowed in a straight line, finishing at Winthrops Point, which is at the exact spot that the old railroad bridge now occupies on the river. The first half mile was rowed close to the west shore, and Yale gained an advantage of nearly half her length, and this lead was maintained or slightly increased during the second half mile. For the next mile, the course led along the edge of the channel so that the west crew was rowing directly in the channel and the east crew for most of this mile was wholly out of the channel, and for a short distance on shallow flats and in eelgrass. The Yale coxswain was said to have steered badly and taken his boat far over to the east shore. Anyhow Yale lost twelve seconds in the second mile. At this point Harvard in effect won the race, for, being well in the channel and observing Yale falling behind, she put on additional steam and quickly took the lead, being perhaps three lengths ahead at the two-mile flag. From this point on, the Yale crew gradually gained on Harvard, and towards the end of the race cut down the latter's lead quite materially.

There were at this time only single flags at intervals of half a mile, and not the three flags as at present to form two lanes for the crews to follow. The only rule then was that each crew should keep on its own side of the single line of flags.

After leaving the Navy Yard the Yale crew swung gradually to the east in order to follow the channel. This proceeding doubtless gave her in her turn somewhat faster water than her rival. She gained rapidly during the third mile.

It has been said by prejudiced observers that if the finish point had been a quarter of a mile farther down Yale would have caught Harvard. There is no doubt that the Harvard crew, owing in part doubtless to Yale's rapid approach in the fast current of the channel and also to the lack of experience of the new man rowing bow, lost its form to a considerable extent in this mile, and more or less went to pieces, and the faster Yale came up on them, the more acute became the danger of their getting panic-stricken, but towards the end they got together again and succeeded in holding their lead. The official time for the Harvard crew was given out as 20 minutes 47½ seconds, and for Yale 20 minutes 50½ seconds, but men standing at the finish line stated that there was not more than 30 or 40 feet between the sterns of the two boats.

The following year rules were made to compel each crew to pass close to each half-mile flag, by adding at each of these points two additional flags, inside of which the boats must pass. On such a course as the Thames River, with one, and in places even two comparatively narrow winding channels and a wide stretch of mud flats, partially uncovered at very low water, some prescribed course was absolutely necessary in order to compel the two crews to race together over the same part of the river, and not wander off in search of faster currents.

The Yale rowing authorities generally considered the result of the Varsity race to be inconclusive as a test for their new rigging and oars, and their so-called American professional style of rowing. They stated and doubtless believed that the Yale crew lost the race in the second mile because of bad steering. The coxswain was blamed for taking their boat through eelgrass and over flats at the time when the Harvard crew was rapidly passing by Yale and steering the correct course. There was much disputing at the time as to the facts, and surely after forty years no verdict can be final. Robert J. Cook alone among Yale supporters maintained in print that Harvard won because of her better style and form, in spite of the superior power and physique of the Yale crew.

Whatever the facts as to steering may be, it is certain that the Harvard supporters had a feeling that their crew had been very fortunate, since they had put in an untrained substitute just before the race, and especially since the official times showed that Yale rowed every mile but the second faster than Harvard. One of the Harvard Societies, in a theatrical performance the next year expressed their sentiments, however, in the following lines:

> The little boys in blue
> Came to see what they could do;
> And many were the things
> That they said, said, said.
> But it was not any use,
> Eel-grass was not an excuse;
> They were walloped by the
> Little boys in red, red, red.

The Harvard crew contained five men who rowed in the University crew of the year before — one man was now a Senior, three of them Juniors, one a Sophomore—while the three remaining men came out of the '84 Freshman crew. The men making up the Yale crew were chiefly from the Junior class.

The style of rowing of the Harvard crew was somewhat stiff. They used a very vigorous catch and a rather long body swing, with a slide not more than twelve inches in length. Their recover was under fair control and in this respect they were far superior to Yale.

About the same time the '85 Harvard Freshman crew rowed a return race on Columbia's home waters. The course selected was on the Haarlem River near Mott Haven in New York City. W. A. Bancroft, who had coached the crew, was necessarily at New London looking after the University crew, and the Harvard Freshmen, lost in a great city, suffered ignominious defeat, finishing fifteen seconds behind Columbia. Since that time the Harvard Varsity and Freshman crews have rowed their final races on the same water.

Harvard 1882 Crew

W. W. MUMFORD, '84	(165)	S. I. HUDGENS, '84	(186)
Bow		W. CHALFANT, '82	(177)
F. L. SAWYER, '83	(167)	C. P. CURTIS, Jr., '83	(161)
R. P. PERKINS, '84	(175)	Stroke	
C. M. HAMMOND, '83	(178)	S. P. SANGER, '83	(90)
E. A. S. CLARKE, '84	(174)	Coxswain	

Average weight 171½ pounds.

Yale 1882 Crew

H. R. FLANDERS, '85	(161)	W. H. HYNDMAN, '84	(182)
Bow		C. B. STORRS, '82	(182)
J. R. PARROTT, '83	(182)	H. T. FOLSOM, '83	(161)
F. W. ROGERS, '83	(172)	Stroke	
N. T. GUERNSEY, L. S.	(176)	D. R. PLESSNER, '85	(86)
L. K. HULL, '83	(180)	Coxswain	

Average weight 176 pounds.

A controversy of great bitterness arose over the fact that the postponed Harvard–Columbia University race never actually took place.

[12]

At four o'clock on the afternoon of Monday, July 3d, the Columbia crew drew up to the start, and was sent over the four miles alone by Mr. R. C. Watson, Harvard '69, who had been selected as referee, and had doubtless been previously notified by Columbia's coach at what hour the crew would be ready. Later Mr. Watson awarded the race to Columbia by default.

In this connection the following announcement was made under date of July 7, 1882, Boston, Massachusetts, and sent to Columbia:

We, the undersigned, graduates and friends of Harvard University, hereby wish to express our entire approval of the decision of the Referee, R. C. Watson, in regard to the race appointed to be rowed between Columbia and Harvard on July 3rd at New London.

We also wish to express our complete disapproval of the course pursued by the Harvard crew in regard to the above race. And finally we wish to express our deep regret for the injustice that has been done the Columbia crew, and our sincere hope that the pleasant relations heretofore existing between Harvard and Columbia may continue unbroken in the future.

Signed:

ALEX. AGASSIZ, '55

S. D. BUSH, '71

R. B. GREENOUGH, '59

REGINALD GRAY, '75

ARTHUR W. HOOPER, '80

J. COLLINS WARREN, '63

W. C. LORING, '72

ROBERT C. HOOPER, '72

WM. FARNSWORTH, '77

W. B. BACON, Jr., '77

WALTER TRIMBLE, '79

CHARLES FAIRCHILD, '58

LOUIS CURTIS, '70

WENDELL GOODWIN, '74

FRANCIS C. LOWELL, '76

ROBERT H. GARDINER, Jr., '76

HENRY PARKMAN, '70

D. B. FAY, '81

N. G. REED, '71

HARCOURT AMORY, '76

JOSEPH S. COOLIDGE, '49

ROBERT S. PEABODY, '66

E. C. Perkins, '66

T. Nelson, '66

James Lawrence, '74

F. W. Lawrence, '61

Theodore Chase, '53

A. Hemenway, '75

Robert G. Shaw, '60

Arthur Rotch, '71

George W. West, '72

J. Murray Forbes, '66

W. Lawrence Sprague, '71

George B. Shattuck, '63

Henry Lee, '36

I. T. Burr, Jr., '79

William Boott, '24

G. S. Dabney, '63

F. C. Loring, '63

F. L. Higginson, '63

Joseph B. Warner, '69

Moses Williams, Jr., '68

Thomas Lee, '79

Robert Bacon, '80

H. R. Horton, '70

John S. Linzee, '77

Charles A. Prince, '73

Francis Peabody, Jr., L. S.

C. C. Jackson, '63

N. H. Stone, '75

Alden P. Loring, '69

T. Parsons, '70

and thirty others.

This declaration clearly demonstrates the intense interest taken by the graduates and their desire to set a high standard of good sportsmanship.

It seems not unreasonable to wonder why the first paragraph commending the referee was inserted, as no one could question that that official had acted entirely impartially, as his position demanded. He could only call off the race at the request of both crews, and the presence of Columbia and the absence of Harvard would seem to have left him no alternative but to act as he did.

Such evidence as has come down to us hardly appears to justify either this wholesale condemnation of Harvard or so unqualified an apology to Columbia. The whole declaration, which was probably drawn without a careful examination of the facts, well illustrates the uncompromising attitude of the graduates towards undergraduates in those days.

The story in brief was that the Columbia coxswain, Edmund Benjamin of New York City, was drowned on Friday, the day before that fixed for the Harvard–Columbia race. Columbia did not make any communication to Harvard until the following Monday, when her representatives announced that because of the funeral the race could not be rowed before Wednesday the 28th. As Harvard was to row Yale on Friday the 30th, she declined to row Columbia on the 28th, but agreed to row on Monday the 3d of July, at noon. This time was fixed to enable the members of the crew to get back to Boston on the afternoon train. On the day after the Yale race Columbia's representatives officially declined to row at noon. The reason they gave was that the tide would be too slow at that hour to enable them to equal the records made by either Harvard or Yale in their race the day before.

Such a reason for changing the hour agreed on, combined with the obvious fact that the Harvard crew had acted remarkably well by Columbia, seems in itself sufficient ground for criticizing Columbia's and not Harvard's sportsmanship. Harvard might well have insisted that Columbia row the race before the funeral, on Monday, June 26th, with a new coxswain, or even have suggested their giving the race up entirely as a mark of respect to their friend.

This unqualified expression of disapproval by the graduates and by the public which naturally followed such a lead, must have fallen upon the surprised Harvard crew with the suddenness of a bombshell, for they had left New London publicly after a final conference between representatives of both crews, with the distinct understanding that the race was off, since Columbia had finally and definitely refused to row at the time previously agreed on. Their only mistake appears to have been that they did not see to it that this conference was held in the presence of the referee, and that he was then made to understand that both crews had agreed that there should be no race.

1883

Harvard won by twenty-one boat lengths

Hammond '83 was reëlected captain of the crew after the '82 race. He had been a St. Paul's School boy. At this period St. Paul's School at Concord, New Hampshire, was the only preparatory school where rowing was carried on as an organized sport. There baseball was not encouraged and such football as there was consisted of interclass games in the fall. The real athletic activities of the boys were divided between rowing and cricket. About thirty boys rowed in the interclub boats until eight-oared shells were introduced in 1890, after which time the number largely increased. Until other schools took up rowing in the nineties, St. Paul's graduates were the only boys who entered Harvard, Yale, or Columbia with any previous rowing experience. Although the rowing at St. Paul's was crude and the boys came to their chosen colleges without having acquired any special skill or real proficiency, they did furnish several Freshman and University crew captains and provided an important nucleus around which the crews of these colleges were developed. Several members of both Harvard and Yale crews of '82 and '83 were St. Paul's boys.

As usual after a victory, the management started out to develop the '83 crew on as nearly as possible the same lines as the winning crew of the previous year. All of the men who rowed in the '82 Harvard crew against Yale returned to College, with the exception of Chalfant '82, who had rowed at No. 7.

[17]

Yale also had practically the same material for its crew as the year before, and unconvinced that their system or method of rowing and rigging was wrong merely because the Harvard crew had defeated them by 40 feet in four miles, they decided to try over again the experiment that had reached what they considered inconclusive results the year before. The Yale crew was coached and directed by the same captain, Louis K. Hull, class of '83, and the same professional oarsman, M. F. Davis, the inventor of the long boat rigged in pairs, the "leg-o'-mutton" oars, a new form of oarlock, and various other mechanical devices intended to give increased speed.

Mr. William A. Bancroft, class of '78, stroke of the winning crews of '77, '78, and '79—better known among Harvard men of his day as "Foxey" Bancroft—at this time Colonel of the Seventh Massachusetts Volunteer Militia, was again appointed coach. Owing to his military connections, he had consciously or unconsciously introduced various military terms into the coaching vocabulary, some of which have remained with us ever since. Colonel Bancroft always labored with a view to having his pupils attain absolute uniformity of style, and required them to adopt an erect military bearing, resulting in a rather marked rigidity of muscles in rowing. His teaching was based upon the so-called English stroke as taught at Eton, and none of his crews were permitted to row more strokes to the minute than they could execute properly and with a view to perfect control of the recover. On the pull-through the men were drilled to lift their bodies with a violent heave at the beginning of the stroke, holding their slides rigid, but this seemingly impossible feat was done successfully because they were taught to cover their blades gradually; or, in other words, row them into the water so that, as a matter of fact, the blade was not covered until the preliminary heave was finished, and the legs came into full play. The importance of uniformity in this respect was held to be so great that during several weeks of the early training of the '83 crew on the river, and in fact during all of the time that the crew used the heavy working barge — the usual custom in those days when first getting on the water — a rigid rod of hard wood was fastened to the sliding seats, connecting them all together, each seat being firmly screwed thereto, so that all of the men should begin and end their sliding at the same instant of time, and all slide the same distance.

The class races, in which all the four class crews participated, were regularly held in May, and Bancroft this year also coached the Freshman crew and also one or more of the other class crews. These four class crews, together with the University crew, were the only eights the College put on the river. They commonly trained more or less in the fall and rowed regularly through the winter on rowing machines in the gymnasium. The custom was for two of these class crew men to be taken onto the University squad after the class races, and as a rule the limit of the actual contribution the class crews made to the University crew was the two substitutes, who did their practising in a pair-oar after the class races, and accompanied the eight to New London. This year, however, James J. Storrow '85 and William G. Borland '86, a Freshman, were put in the University crew at No. 3 and No. 2 respectively after the class races.

In May it was announced to the great discouragement of the College that Charles P. Curtis, Jr. '83, stroke of the crew, who had rowed in the same seat in both the '81 and '82 Yale races, had injured his hip and would be obliged to give up his seat in the boat. R. P. Perkins '84, who rowed No. 3 in the '82 crew, eventually replaced Curtis at stroke.

When the crew went to New London, the general impression at the College was that it was made up of inferior material and was below the standard of the three crews immediately preceding. In the Columbia race, which was rowed on June 20th over the four-mile course at New London about a week before the Yale race, the Harvard crew showed such excellent form and evidence of ability to row fast that it was suddenly realized that this was an unusually good crew. In this race, Harvard quickly took the lead and defeated Columbia by sixty-five seconds, estimated at over twenty lengths, rowing against a head wind.

The Yale race, which followed a week after, on June 28th, was a procession after the end of the first quarter mile, with Yale rowing 45 strokes to the minute. The same controversy had arisen again owing to the difference in the length of the rival shells as to whether they should be judged at the finish by the bows or by the sterns. The matter was settled by placing a small crimson flag on the tip of Harvard's bow and a similar blue flag at a point on the Yale boat three or four feet back from the bow, which point was to be considered as the actual bow, in judging the start and the winner at the finish line. The basis of this arrangement was to bring the exact centers of the two boats directly opposite each other. The crews rowed down stream against a strong head wind. At the start the long Yale boat, with its little flag to mark its official bow, shot ahead of the Harvard crew and for a minute it looked as though Yale would prove a dangerous opponent. The Harvard crew, rowing 36 to the minute, overhauled its rival before they had rowed a quarter of a mile; and from that point, at a stroke of 30 to 34 to the minute, rowed rapidly away from Yale, defeating the latter by about a minute and a quarter. Harvard's time was 25 minutes 46½ seconds and Yale's 26 minutes 59 seconds.

The men in this Harvard crew were unusually well together, the three stern men were especially smooth and had excellent control of their recover, showing little evidence of any marked heave with the shoulders at the catch, and it would have taken an unusually good crew to defeat them. It has gone down in rowing annals as probably the fastest of the crews turned out by either Harvard or Yale during the four years from 1880 to 1884 inclusive.

The Yale crew admirably illustrated the futility of the theory that the more strokes the crew could row to the minute, the faster it would go. This theory has constantly cropped up in eight-oar rowing in this country under the title of the "professional stroke" and was known in England as the "American stroke" and even at Cornell was looked upon as gospel until a Cornell crew was defeated at the Henley Regatta of 1895. Mr. C. F. Francis, of Troy, N. Y., who acted as manager for Cornell in England on that occasion, frequently stated, in interviews, that he was sure Cornell would win the Henley Regatta because it was always able to row the Henley course as laid out on Lake Cayauga without letting the stroke fall befow 50 to the minute. After 1883 Harvard never competed in a regular race with another college whose crew ignored the old English principle that control of the recover in an eight was essential to its speed, but for many years a misconception existed in the public mind over the coaching of college crews by professional oarsmen, and it was incorrectly believed that a college crew coached by a professional oarsman necessarily rowed like the Yale '82 and '83 crews.

In 1880 and for ten years thereafter, Harvard used paper boats constructed in Troy, N. Y. The skin or surface of these boats consisted of a mixture of paper pulp and shellac, the latter being used to stiffen the composition and make it impervious to water. The rest of the braces, gunwales, keels, etc., were of wood, as in the cedar shells. Eight-oared wooden shells imported from England in the late '70's were used as the models for these paper boats, and as they appeared to be no heavier than wooden boats of the same size, and were thought to be fully as elastic and to ride as well on the surface of water under suitable racing conditions, their availability and lower cost rendered their use almost universal amongst American colleges at this time.

As the only test of merit in college boat racing appears to rest on success, the devices used by the Harvard crew in the '83 race were accepted in the rowing world as the correct ones, and those used by Yale as the wrong ones; and because Yale this year used a wooden boat, "leg-o'-mutton" oars, and was seated in pairs, for several years thereafter wooden eight-oared shells were generally under the same ban that condemned the other devices and eccentricities that characterized the '83 Yale crew. As the crew was supposedly coached by a professional oarsman who not only permitted but seemingly taught the men to rush the recover, an idea prevailed, at least at Cambridge and New Haven, that all professional oarsmen were unsafe as coaches for eight-oared crews.

The '86 Freshman race between Harvard and Columbia was rowed at New London on June 27th, the day before the Harvard–

Yale University race, over the last two miles of the four-mile course. Harvard won the race with comparative ease by a margin of 19 seconds, equal to five or six boat lengths. Harvard class of '86 never after figured conspicuously in rowing, and none of the men who rowed against Columbia in this race, nor any '86 man except Borland, ever attained to a seat in a University crew in a Harvard–Yale race.

Harvard 1883 Crew

W. W. Mumford, '84	(167)	F. L. Sawyer, '83	(167)
Bow		C. M. Belshaw, '83	(162)
W. G. Borland, '86	(169)	R. P. Perkins, '84	(181)
J. J. Storrow, '85	(155)	Stroke	
C. M. Hammond, '83	(179)	S. P. Sanger, '83	(98)
E. A. S. Clarke, '84	(181)	Coxswain.	

Average weight 169 lbs.

Yale 1883 Crew

H. R. Flanders, '85	(162)	W. H. Hyndman, '84	(180)
Bow		F. W. Rogers, '83	(169)
J. R. Parrott, '83	(176)	H. T. Folsom, '83	(168)
L. K. Hull, '83	(177)	Stroke	
N. T. Guernsey, L. S.	(172)	D. B. Tucker, '83	(107)
F. G. Peters, '86	(174)	Coxswain	

Average weight 172 lbs.

1884

Yale won by five boat lengths

E. A. S. Clarke, class of '84, of New York, was elected captain of the University crew immediately after the '83 race, but resigned his position when the fall term opened, and was succeeded by Robert Patterson Perkins '84, also of New York City, who had rowed stroke of the '83 University crew.

As usual after a victory over Yale, the crew management entered upon the new season with few or no changes in the coaching or the system of work. All of the members of the '83 crew, with the exception of No. 7, were available, but the Freshman crew of the previous summer, which defeated the Columbia '86 Freshman crew at New London offered but little promising material for the University eight. As usual, the major part of the training previous to the breaking up of the ice in the spring consisted of daily work on the hydraulic rowing machines in the gymnasium, followed by a run up North Avenue at least as far as the railroad station, usually covering in all two or three miles.

Little attempt at fall rowing on the river was made by any of the University or class crew organizations this year.

On October 24th, so-called "scratch races" were arranged to be held in front of the boat house between crews drawn by lot, made up of rowing men in the three upper classes. The boat house was located on the north side of the Charles River about 400 yards below the site of the present Weld boat house. It was supported on piles in the mud close to the bank, with two balco-

[24]

Class Races on Charles River Basin. The Finish

From *Harvard Lampoon* of 1885

nies ornamenting the front, one above the other, capable of holding a large number of men. As the spectators congregated on these balconies on this occasion to witness the "scratch races," the weight proved too great for the piles supporting one of the corners. With their collapse over one hundred men were precipitated into the mud of the Charles River, the tide being low at the time. Some ten Harvard men were injured, several of them quite severely, and this accident is notable as being the only serious one that ever occurred in Cambridge in connection with athletic contests. The races were given up.

Colonel Bancroft again in full charge devoted the chief part of his time to coaching the University crew, but he also superintended this year the development of the Junior, Sophomore, and Freshman class crews.

Harvard again had as a preliminary contest the four-mile race with Columbia University, which took place at New London on June 18th, about a week before the race with Yale. Harvard appears at this time to have come to look upon this contest as a practice row of hardly sufficient importance to test the powers of her crew, and the interest in which was too slight to warrant even the running of an observation train by the New London and Northern Railroad. Before two miles of the race were completed, the members of the Harvard crew began to realize that they were not as much superior to Columbia as they had expected, and although Columbia was defeated by a considerable margin, the Harvard management was by no means satisfied with the showing made by their crew. Their rowing was ragged, the men were not together, and that they won was due to the wretched work of the Columbia crew. A radical rearrangement

ROBERT P. PERKINS, '84, IN HIS SENIOR YEAR

he was immensely superior to every other man this year on the river. Bryant at No. 7 supported him surprisingly well in view of the fact that he had been trained to row only on the port side of the boat, but long before the end of the race the rest of the crew, not being well together and, moreover, largely new to their positions, threw much more of the burden upon stroke than any one man could possibly carry.

The race was rowed down stream under fast conditions about 2:45 in the afternoon of June 26th. The start was rather unequal, as Harvard did not appear to be ready and Yale was off and had an advantage of nearly half a length before Harvard was well under way. The boats maintained these relative positions for about half the race, although at one time it looked as if Harvard had succeeded in overhauling Yale. In the last two miles the Harvard crew, although it had been rowing much better than in the Columbia race, showed the effects of the recent shifting of the men. They began to get out of their beat, the rowing became ragged and Yale won the race by seventeen seconds in 20 minutes and 31 seconds, the difference being estimated at five boat lengths. Robert J. Cook, Yale '76, coached the Yale crew, and its form was not unlike that of Harvard, none of the peculiarities of the Yale crews of the two previous seasons being in evidence.

The Harvard and Columbia '87 Freshman crews rowed their race immediately after the University race, over the last two miles of the course. Columbia at once took the lead and won by seven seconds in the rather fast time of 9 minutes 43 seconds. Four of this Harvard crew and five of the Columbia rowed against each other again two years later in their respective University crews.

With this race ended Colonel William A. Bancroft's, '78, active connection with Harvard rowing, which had lasted almost uninterruptedly for ten years, and with his retirement ended one continuous and settled policy in the coaching which had been maintained for the same period.

As a Sophomore in 1876 he had stroked Harvard's first eight-oared crew at Springfield on the Connecticut River in the first four-mile Harvard–Yale race. Robert J. Cook stroked the Yale eight in this race and Yale won. Foxey Bancroft was captain and again stroke in 1877 at the same place, when Harvard won. The next year the first race over the four-mile New London course was an easy victory for Harvard, Bancroft being again stroke and captain. In 1879, while in the Law School, he once more, and for the last time, stroked a Harvard crew against Yale. The race was rowed late in the day and it was nearly dark when Harvard crossed the finish line. Yale was literally not in sight as the light was too faint for the spectators to make her out, still rowing and still far away up the course. Of the four subsequent University crews that he coached, two of them, the '82 and '83 crews, won from Yale, the second by almost as large a margin as his own famous '79 crew.

Harvard 1884 Crew

J. R. Yocom, '85	(168)	S. I. Hudgens, '84	(185)
Bow		W. S. Bryant, '84	(164)
A. Keith, '85	(164)	R. P. Perkins, '84	(179)
J. J. Storrow, Jr., '85	(156)	Stroke	
F. L. Sawyer, L. S.	(167)	C. D. Davis, '84	(100)
W. G. Borland, '86	(168)	Coxswain	

Average weight 169 lbs.

[28]

WILLIAM A. BANCROFT, '78, IN 1882

Yale 1884 Crew

R. S. Storrs, '85 Bow	(159)	J. R. Parrott, L. S.	(180)
		J. F. Scott, '84	(166)
C. B. Hobbs, '85	(169)	H. R. Flanders, '85	(158)
H. W. Patten, '86	(164)	Stroke	
A. Cowles, Jr., '86	(169)	L. E. Cadwell, '86	(84)
F. G. Peters, '86	(179)	Coxswain	

Average weight 168 lbs.

1885

Harvard won by twenty-two boat lengths

James J. Storrow, Jr., class of '85, of Boston, was elected captain of the crew immediately after the '84 race.

Storrow found himself in difficulties with the Faculty Committee on Athletics before the fall term was many days old.

The Faculty began two or three years before to attempt officially to regulate and control undergraduate athletic activities. They had appointed a special committee on athletics from their own body, consisting of Professors Charles Eliot Norton, John Williams White, and Assistant Professor Dudley A. Sargent, the director of the gymnasium, to investigate and make recommendations to the Faculty, and had also invested these professors with a certain amount of direct authority.

At first the students had been inclined to ridicule these efforts. They celebrated the Committee in verse:

Rub a dub dub, three men in a tub, all bound for Utopia City;
A sage, a reformer, a trapeze performer, and that's our Athletic Committee.

The last title was derived from Doctor Sargent's great skill as a gymnast and especially his ability to balance himself in the flying trapeze while seated in a rocking chair.

Early in 1884 the undergraduates discovered that the Faculty was very much in earnest. It published certain resolutions it had passed regarding athletics, containing amongst others some of the following provisions:

PROFESSOR CHARLES ELIOT NORTON
Chairman of the Athletic Committee, 1882–85

That all coaches must be appointed by the Athletic Committee.

That no professional should be employed.

That none of the teams or crews should take part in any contest whatever except with the teams or crews of other colleges.

That no student should compete for more than four years.

That no boat race should be for a longer distance than three miles.

As a result of student mass meetings and further discussions back and forth, the Faculty reconsidered immediate or drastic action. The Committee on Athletics thereupon proceeded to act with authoritative vigor, on the basis that these Faculty votes were merely expressions of opinion and were not orders. They now directed that football be discontinued as too brutal for a recognized sport, and as a result no intercollegiate football games were played in 1885.

In October, 1884, the Athletic Committee notified Captain Storrow that no person would be allowed to coach the University or class crews without the written approval of a certain Graduate Committee on Boating, and two weeks later he received another communication, this time signed by Edward N. Fenno '68, R. C. Watson '69, and N. G. Read '71, "Graduate Committee on Boating," stating that under authority vested in them they wished that no paid coach should be allowed to train any of the crews and specifically that they did not approve of the employment of Colonel Bancroft.

Captain Storrow appealed from this decision to the Faculty Committee on Athletics, and in reply received a letter from that committee which instructed him "to discontinue immediately the employment of Colonel Bancroft as coach." Owing to the uncertainty that existed in their minds, with which of the two committees this unwelcome idea originated, the crew, or more strictly speaking the candidates for the crew, regarded both committees with an equal and impartial resentment, as exercising an arbitrary and in the case of the rowing committee an usurped authority.

For several years there had existed a Graduate Committee on Rowing, whose method of selection had been rather indefinite and whose functions had been wholly advisory. Its members had been used as Harvard's officials in the races and its counsel had been sought by captains. Professor Alexander Agassiz previously acted as its chairman, but he had resigned just before this, and Mr. R. C. Watson had assumed his place. This committee had always kept itself in the background, until thus put upon the stage by the Athletic Committee. The action of the captain in going over its head through his direct appeal to the Faculty Athletic Committee made it realize that its further usefulness even in a friendly advisory capacity had now ended, so it resigned in a body, and no successors were appointed.

This incident had a far-reaching effect on Harvard rowing, and was the cause of much of the lack of sympathy that existed for the next fifteen years in rowing circles between the undergraduates and a large and influential body of former Harvard oarsmen. This lack of sympathy, amounting at times almost to open hostility, which arose from undergraduate jealousy of assumption of official authority by any graduate committee, had a serious effect upon the success of our crews. The argument on the other side was that if the undergraduates were unable to manage their crews successfully, they must consent to receive advice and assistance from those older and wiser than themselves. Up to this time at Harvard, since eight-oared racing began, there had been no serious disagreement on the question of coach, but dating from the order for the dismissal of Colonel Bancroft there existed for several years a constant and openly expressed difference of opinion as to conduct and policy.

Captain Storrow tried to find a coach from among the old available rowing men, for apparently he was restricted to such as could afford to give their time without pay. To add to his difficulties he had to create a new crew out of untried material.

He started almost entirely with such material as was furnished by the '87 Freshman crew, which had been defeated by the Columbia Freshman crew in June at New London in a two-mile race. The feeling of the rowing men was so bitter against the Athletic Committee, for depriving them of Colonel Bancroft's services by a mere order and without sufficiently consulting with the captain or any undergraduates, that sentiment was strongly against accepting any coach favored either by the Athletic Committee or by the former Rowing Committee.

The '84 class crew, which easily won the class races the year before, had been coached by George Faulkner, a professional oarsman of considerable local fame. Faulkner had rowed bow of a professional four-oared crew which had figured successfully in regattas in various parts of the country; he had acted as coach of this crew, and had also been accustomed to give more or less rowing instruction to a number of well-known professional scullers. He considered the style of stroke used by Edward Hanlon, of Toronto, Canada, who for ten years held the position of sculling champion of the world, as the model for all oarsmen, and taught a carefully controlled recover, firm catch, and a hard finish, with stroke as long as possible. Captain Storrow frequently sought his advice in matters connected with the coaching of the crew, and finally decided to adopt entirely Faulkner's ideas.

It appeared to be unwise to consult the Faculty Committee on Athletics as to employing a coach either with or without pay. It might or might not approve of Faulkner but it had forbidden the employment of any coach without the approval of the Graduate Committee on Rowing. But there now existed no such committee. The Athletic Committee could hardly prevent Faulkner from rowing in his single where the crew was practising, and suggestions and advice given at such times gradually led to his occasionally taking out members of the crew in a pair-oar. By degrees he increased the time he gave to the work and sat occasionally in the eight or rode in the bow of the launch although in the early part of the season he made but little use of the launch, which had always been employed by Colonel Bancroft, but usually did most of his coaching while rowing in his single or from a seat in the boat in place of one of the regular men.

R. F. A. Penrose '84 who rowed No. 6 in the Senior class crew the previous spring and had returned to College to take a special graduate course, was, in April, placed at stroke of the University crew, Captain Storrow rowing at No. 7.

The crew went to New London an entirely unknown quantity, and the feeling in the College was that some experiment in rowing was being attempted, which would probably fail, as the Yale professional experiment had failed two years previously.

Harvard, '85, University Crew at New London

HARVARD, '85, CREW AT QUARTERS

Left to right: John Smith, the janitor and boat rigger; George Faulkner; Yocom, '85, No. 5; F. Remington, '87, substitute; T. Q. Browne, '88, Coxswain; T. P. Burgess, '87, No. 3; G. S. Mumford, '87, No. 4; H. W. Keyes, '87, Bow; James J. Storrow, '85, No. 7; W. A. Brooks, Jr., '87, No. 6; R. A. F. Penrose, Graduate, Stroke; J. J. Colony, '85, No. 2; R. C. Watson, '69; W. Alexander, '87; L. E. Sexton, '84; Evert J. Wendell, '82; a visitor.

The usual four-mile race with the Columbia University crew, scheduled for a week before the Yale race, proved such a complete walk-over for the Harvard crew that the rowing enthusiasts suddenly awoke to the fact that something out of the ordinary was going on at the Harvard quarters. The race was rowed down stream against a head wind and the time made was slow. The Columbia crew was so far behind at the first half-mile flag that the Harvard crew dropped to a slow stroke and the race appeared to give them little further anxiety.

In spite of their speed, which was proved by several short trial rows over measured distances, the crew was not in first-class physical condition, the men had lost much weight and were down very fine indeed. The pernicious theory existed then and for a long time afterwards, that no man should drink more than six glasses of liquid in the twenty-four hours. A man might lose five or six pounds in an afternoon's row equivalent to ten or twelve glasses of water, but no conscientious member of a crew dreamed of compromising with his thirst or with the hot sun, but stuck to his limited allowance of drink and lost weight accordingly. Between the first of June and the day of the Yale race this crew lost nearly fifteen pounds per man, and had the Columbia race been a close enough contest to test their powers of endurance, their condition in the Yale race would have proved a much more serious matter.

Mr. R. C. Watson '69 spent several days at the Harvard quarters after the Columbia race, and his presence was welcomed by the crew, for as a whole, old Harvard oarsmen were conspicuous by their absence from the Harvard camp.

After beating Columbia by nearly two minutes, equal to three-eighths of a mile, the Harvard crew the following week defeated the Yale crew, which was substantially the same crew that had beaten Harvard the previous year, the margin between the two at the finish being about a quarter of a mile.

The Yale race was rowed down stream about noon, Harvard having the west course. A strong head wind blew up the course. The Yale coach, Robert J. Cook, had given out interviews in the newspapers that the race would be a repetition of the '83 race, only that the professionally coached Harvard crew would be perhaps in the lead at first, but that this time Yale with its proper "English" form would soon row its rival down. His interview emphasized so strongly the evils of employing for hire a professional coach, who even rowed clad in a crimson jersey in the Harvard eight, that the Harvard Faculty took notice of the matter and despatched a committee consisting of two of their own number to investigate such a scandalous proceeding. These professors found Faulkner at the Harvard quarters, but convinced themselves that the situation had been grossly exaggerated, and they apparently so reported back to the Faculty, for no action was taken.

Contrary to Mr. Cook's professed opinion, the form shown in the race by the Harvard crew was so much the superior that Yale lost ground steadily from start to finish, except at the two-mile point, when a launch carrying a large blue flag crossed Harvard's bow and nearly swamped the shell. Harvard's time was 25 minutes 15½ seconds, and Yale's 26 minutes 30 seconds.

Captain Storrow had created a new era in college rowing. He had developed a crew out of only average material which was incomparably faster than any competitor. The reason for this lay in the central fact that under the stroke used the men were successfully taught to combine what was best in professional rowing with the correct principles of the so-called English stroke. In some later years Harvard boating enthusiasts failed to do justice to the unique position and the achievements of her '85 University crew, but not so with the Yale rowing authorities. For years afterwards Yale coaches openly stated that the style of Penrose, the Harvard stroke, was nearly perfect, and succeeding Yale crews were taught by Cook to row as nearly as possible as he did; and likewise at Columbia University a new era in rowing was inaugurated to date from their overwhelming defeat by Harvard in 1885.

Of all athletic sports, rowing appears to be the most conservative. The football game as played in 1885 was so unlike the game of thirty years later that there hardly exists any point of resemblance except in the shape of the ball, and even position of the men on the field before beginning to play is different. In baseball, too, the change brought about by the use of gloves, the catcher's mask, and the great improvements in pitching in the course of thirty years have altered the aspect and the character of the game.

But in eight-oared college rowing there has been no such change during the thirty years or more since 1885. The model of the boat, the length of the outrigger, the oarlock, the oar, even the sliding seat and stretcher of 1885 are practically identical with those of today. The measurements used in connection with seating the individual men differ but little. Captain Storrow made a great effort to have his men rigged properly, so that each man would be in a position to do his most effective work, and the length of slide which he determined upon as the correct one, which averaged nineteen inches, is about the same as used by American eight-oared crews today. Previous to 1885 the slide was never over twelve to fourteen inches in length, except in the Yale '82 and '83 crews. By an odd coincidence the English University crews lengthened their slides from about twelve inches to sixteen this same year.

It is probably no exaggeration to state that no eight-oared crew representing any American college since that time has left so deep an impress on the history and teaching of rowing at Harvard and Yale as the Harvard University crew of 1885.

The Freshman '88 crews of Harvard and Columbia rowed their race over the last two miles of the course the day before the Harvard–Yale University race. The Harvard Freshmen had been coached by Mumford '87, one of the members of the University crew, and showed considerable speed. They rowed away from Columbia with apparent ease, defeating them by about fifteen boat lengths.

Harvard 1885 Crew

H. W. KEYES, '87	(163)	W. A. BROOKS, Jr., '87	(165)
Bow		J. J. STORROW, Jr., '85	(153)
J. J. COLONY, '85	(159)	R. F. A. PENROSE, Gr.	(162)
T. P. BURGESS, '87	(175)	Stroke	
G. S. MUMFORD, '87	(145)	T. Q. BROWNE, '88	(96)
J. R. YOCOM, '85	(173)	Coxswain	

Average weight 162½ lbs.

Rowing Room in Hemenway Gymnasium in 1885

Bow, Brooks, '87; Cabot, '86; Keyes, '87; Colony, '85; Yocom, '85; Storrow, '85;
Burgess, '87; Mumford, '87, Stroke

Yale 1885 Crew

C. S. Dodge, '85	(159)	J. R. Parrott, L. S.	(180)
Bow		F. G. Peters, '86	(184)
R. S. Storrs, '85	(162)	H. R. Flanders, '85	(163)
H. W. Patten, '86	(175)	Stroke	
C. B. Hobbs, '85	(171)	L. E. Cadwell, '86	(84)
A. Cowles, Jr., '86	(170)	Coxswain	

Average weight 170 lbs.

And now for a brief period to assume the first person.

It was an evening in the autumn of 1884 and a meeting was being held in Jim Storrow's room in Little's Block. There were present some of us who had rowed in the Freshman crew against Columbia the previous June, also Yocom '85, who had rowed in our Varsity crew in the Yale race after three days' previous practice, and I think John Colony '85, who had never rowed at all. Captain Storrow had called us together to tell us we had been forbidden by the Athletic Committee to have Foxey Bancroft coach us, and the question to be decided was what we should do next. We felt at the time as if the Athletic Committee had taken up perhaps a minute or two of its time from more important matters in order to send us word that the one rowing graduate who was by all odds the most prominent of his day, a man who had coached four successive University crews with a result fifty per cent successful, must give us no further help of any kind, and that there its duty and responsibility ended unless something else was discovered to disapprove of and forbid.

In gloomy silence we received the judgment and waited rather hopelessly for some suggestion from Jim Storrow. We might get Charles Curtis '83, who was then in the Law School, but that an excessive modesty prompted him to reject such suggestion as to himself. No graduate was available in whom we had confidence. Seemingly we were forbidden to pay a professional coach, so we did not even consider that possible resource. Finally it was decided that we should coach ourselves.

One Sunday morning in the following June, 1885, we met at the boat house. It was a few days before we were to leave for the quarters at New London. We were breaking Sunday regulations in order to test our speed against an eight of well-known professional scullers and oarsmen who volunteered to race us from good nature and for the fun of watching us struggle after them on the short stretch of water in front of the boat house.

Dick Penrose '84, who was studying for a Ph.D. in Geology, was our stroke. He had rowed in his class crew the year before. Captain Storrow rowed No. 7, and Yocom '85 and Colony '85 were at No. 5 and No. 2 respectively. The other four of us came from the slow '87 Freshman crew of the year before. We had all rowed in a light pair-oar with George Faulkner, whose coaching had opened our eyes to new possibilities in rowing form and speed, and by this time we had become conscious that we actually felt at home in the shell. We were surprised to find that the boat did not roll on the recover, the stroke seemed yards long and not a bit hurried, and that somehow although such of the old oarsmen as noticed us or referred to us did so in terms of more or less modified disapproval, we ourselves felt that there must be some mistake in

FROM A CARTOON DRAWN FOR THE *Lampoon* IN 1884 AND NEVER PUBLISHED

their estimate, that it could not be that we were so altogether hopelessly slow.

This Sunday morning was intensely hot, and as we looked at the professional eight rowing up and down for practice, their boat seemed to respond to efforts of its crew with a surprising amount of life and "jump." We tried them for three or four stretches, none of which were over half a mile long, and found them slower than we had expected. They were not able to keep up with us. They too were surprised and anything but satisfied, although their final decision was that we rowed about as well as they did and were better together. It was suggested that they race us again after they had a couple of weeks' practice together, a not unreasonable request, but one altogether impracticable for that particular season.

When we backed up to the stake boat for the Columbia race, we were still wondering whether we could possibly be all wrong and the men at the Yale quarters and at the Columbia quarters, as well as the general sentiment about us in Cambridge and Boston, be right in regarding us as a hopelessly misguided proposition. Harvard was usually expected to beat Columbia without excessive effort, but this time even Columbia was generally expected to defeat this unfortunate Harvard crew with its twenty-inch slides and other adaptations from professional scullers, although it was admitted that for a professionally coached crew our recover was under excellent control.

After I had counted six strokes, I looked over directly to the right, but did not see Columbia at first. She did not appear to be there where she should have been. I became reassured that it must really be a race, however, because the referee did not recall us. Evidently Columbia was slow in getting started and I reflected that we ought to take all possible advantage of this fact and get well ahead at the half-mile flag. I saw nothing more of her and at the finish we seemed to wait an interminable time before our rivals in their turn crossed the line. It was one of the few periods of waiting in my life that I thoroughly enjoyed.

The verdict at the Yale quarters was interesting. They pronounced us clearly faster at any rate for a short distance than their own crew; that we had mastered some secret which they too could learn within the few days before their race with us. Instead of being a despised and neglected crew, we were subject after the Columbia race to many attentions, some of them pleasant and some not. The Yale crew and its instructor, Bob Cook, in their launch, followed at close range all our motions whenever we went out in our shell, and we began to suspect ourselves to be actually illustrating how a crew ought to row.

I believe the Yale crew was as fast for a mile or so as it was the year before, but in their physical condition the men did not look quite as good. In the race we did not run away from them quite as rapidly as we did from Columbia a week earlier and I always suspected that we were ourselves by this time far too fine to stand a hard four-mile contest. I know that speaking for myself I was mighty glad to observe that the Yale crew at the end of the first mile was so far behind as to give me an excuse for taking things easy.

The newspapers after the race referred to us as Storrow's crew, and our style as Storrow's stroke, and with entire justice, for the whole season had been planned and worked out by Captain Storrow alone. I could not but wonder whether the Athletic

Committee the previous autumn in the solitary instance when it appeared to show an interest in rowing affairs had not unintentionally done us a good turn. Thanks to Captain Storrow, to Faulkner, and to a certain amount of intelligence on our own part, what had looked the previous fall like a perfectly hopeless situation had developed in June into a veritable triumph.

1886

Yale won by six boat lengths

George S. Mumford, of the class of '87, from Rochester, N. Y., a graduate of St. Paul's School, was elected captain of the crew immediately after the Harvard–Yale race of '85. This was the third captain in four successive years who came from St. Paul's School, Storrow being the one exception.

All of the members of the '85 crew except No. 7 and stroke presented themselves as candidates for the crew, and the outlook was excellent. George Faulkner was still available as the coach, for he lived in Cambridge, where he was employed as the foreman of gangs of men who unloaded coal schooners and barges at the wharves along the bank of the Charles River. He expressed himself as willing to help in developing the crew in his spare time. No regular application appears to have been made by the captain to obtain permission from the Athletic Committee to use Faulkner as coach. The order of the previous year that the Graduate Committee on Rowing must approve the coach was all very well, but there was no graduate rowing committee to apply to. The fact remains that he was publicly used and no objection was made by the College authorities.

This season Harvard had been prohibited from taking part in intercollegiate football.

The Faculty about this time decided to make a change in its system of regulation of athletics. It abolished its subcommittee on athletics and an Athletic Committee was appointed, consisting of representatives of the Faculty and the undergraduates together with a physician and the director of the gymnasium. It acted largely as a buffer between the students and the College authorities, and so directed athletic activities as to avoid comment by the Faculty, either favorable or otherwise. As a result it was regarded by the undergraduates as a sort of stepfather rather than a sympathetic and helpful parent, and this attitude continued until Professor Ira A. Hollis took the chairmanship in 1897.

In 1890 the present arrangement of a mixed committee of nine was adopted.

When the rowing season on the river opened in the spring, Franklin Remington '87, a substitute of the year before, rowed at stroke, the other vacancy being filled temporarily by one of the men who had rowed on the '88 Freshman crew.

The crew developed very rapidly and showed unusual speed for the early season. It rowed a race about the first of May against two of the class crews, giving one class crew two or three lengths' start over the two-mile course and taking up a second at the end of the first mile, and led both of these crews at the finish.

A professional eight was also organized at this time, made up of several men of national prominence as scullers. A spare eight-oared shell was turned over to them and they practised together for two weeks before giving the University crew a race. Walter Camp in his article on Rowing at Yale in the *Yale Book* published in 1899 referring to this race is quoted as follows:

As a means of comparing the rowing of professionals and college crews, reference may be made to two contests at Boston. Of these rather remarkable races rowed on the Charles River, one late in the seventies, and the other about 1885, the first was between Bancroft's crew and eight of the best oarsmen that could be picked up from about

Boston, practically a professional crew. In that professional crew sat Faulkner, as well as such men as Plaisted, Ross, and Gorkin. The two crews paddled down to the starting-point at Brookline Bridge, and the race was then rowed over the two-mile course. In describing it, an old Harvard oarsman says that when the University Crew had reached the Union Boat House, their professional rivals had already carried the boat into the boat house and were wiping her off. The other contest, of 1885, was between a scratch crew containing Faulkner, Hosmer, Casey, Gorgin, and Kilrane, and others. This time, however, the Harvard Crew defeated the professionals in two miles.

This second contest here referred to was as a matter of fact rowed in May, 1886. The professional eight was made up of Daniel Breen, Bow, Jere Casey, Sylvester Gookin, Richard Gookin, Jake Kilrane, J. Norris, John McKay, George H. Hosmer, stroke. Kilrane was at this time a well-known prize fighter, and shortly after made the fight of seventy-five rounds with the celebrated John L. Sullivan in which he almost succeeded in obtaining the title of World's Champion, and Hosmer, the stroke, ranked with Wallace Ross next to Hanlon among the world's fastest single scullers.

The Harvard crew was made up of Remington '87, stroke; Faulkner, the coach, at No. 7; Mumford '87, No. 6; Burgess '87; Brooks '87; Yocom '85; Colony '85; Butler '88, bow. Keyes '87, the regular No. 7, was temporarily out of the boat because of illness, and Faulkner, although forty-five years of age, took his place. It is probable that Faulkner had much to do with winning the race, as he forced the crew to maintain the stroke at not less than thirty-six and much of the time thirty-eight strokes to the minute, a rather killing pace for most amateurs to hold for two miles.

The contest was extremely close. They were even at the mill dam a mile from the finish, but the professional crew led by twenty feet at Hereford Street. The Harvard crew caught the other just before the finish and won by half a boat length.

At this time the crew was clearly exceedingly fast, although yet a full month before the day fixed for the Yale race, and it was decided to put Penrose, who was still in College as a graduate student, back again in his old position at stroke. It was just here that the lack of close intimate relations between the old Harvard rowing men and the crew management probably cost Harvard dear. Their friendly advice might have served to prevent or modify the radical changes that now followed in the seating of the men in the boat. The event proved that Penrose had begun too late to enable him to get into as good condition and form as on the previous year, and the crew never again came back to the point it had attained before the changes were made.

Upon coming to their quarters at New London it was discovered that the Columbia University crew was rowing exceedingly well. It was composed largely of new men taken chiefly from their '87 Freshman crew and the prospect was regarded with some anxiety.

It was known that the Columbia men had been rigged and trained as nearly as possible on the same lines as Harvard, but it was hardly expected that they could succeed in winning from Harvard this year.

The race was rowed down stream, Harvard having the east or so-called eelgrass course. The early part was entirely satisfactory to Harvard, for she led Columbia at the end of the mile by over a boat length. During the next mile, Columbia gained ten boat lengths or more, eventually defeating the Harvard crew by about six boat lengths. After the race the Harvard coxswain stated that early in the second mile he noticed a lot of driftwood lying directly in Harvard's course, which he avoided by turning sharply in towards shore. It was at this point that Columbia passed Harvard, and made its great gain, recalling a similar experience that Yale suffered in the 1882 race. Whatever the cause, this race resulted in greatly exhausting the strength of the men in the Harvard boat, from which they had not recovered when they came to the Yale race.

The result of this race created a marked sensation in Cambridge. Harvard had been rowing Columbia for several years, winning with perfect regularity, and the race came to be regarded in the College as always a foregone conclusion, perhaps useful as a practice row, but nothing more. To be sure, Yale might beat us, but that Columbia should defeat even our slowest crews was inconceivable. And now a Harvard crew which was supposed to be perhaps the fastest that Harvard had ever put on the water, and supported enthusiastically by the College, had been ignominiously defeated. Such a thing seemed unbelievable.

This year Yale had arranged to have a practice race with the University of Pennsylvania, as an offset to her rival's race with Columbia. This was rowed over the regular four-mile course down stream a few days before the Harvard–Yale race and proved an easy victory for Yale by more than fifteen boat lengths. The Yale crew was clearly much better than the year before. The Yale–University of Pennsylvania race proved to be an annual event for several years.

The presence of both Columbia and Pennsylvania at New London, followed a year later by Cornell, proved the beginning of the present so-called Intercollegiate Regattas, which four years later were shifted to the Poughkeepsie course on the Hudson River.

The Yale race was rowed on July 1st up stream, starting from a point near where the railroad bridge was under construction, and finishing at the usual starting line opposite the Harvard quarters close to the west bank of the river. Because of rough water it had been postponed from the morning and was rowed on very low tide late in the day. Harvard had the west course and backed up to the river's edge close to a huge new railroad embankment just constructed as an approach to the new bridge. Yale was in the channel where the tide proved too strong to permit the anchoring of a stake boat. The start was in consequence rather unsatisfactory. Yale immediately took the lead, which she maintained throughout. In the third mile owing to the low tide Yale found herself in slow water on the east course. Harvard came up rapidly and it looked for a moment as if she might overhaul Yale. This expectation proved futile, although the effort was a creditable one and the boats actually lapped for an instant, but the Yale crew drew away rapidly in the last mile and won by about six boat lengths. The Yale time was 20 minutes 41 seconds and Harvard finished in 21 minutes 5 seconds.

It is probable that the result was due in part to the extremely poor condition of most of the men in the Harvard boat, because of the Columbia race rowed a few days before. Harvard's form, however, at the time of the race was not as good as the year before, although the crew had lost only one man — Storrow, No. 7 — out of the '85 boat. The stroke had shortened somewhat and with it a little more emphasis had been given to an unsightly elbow motion on the beginning of the recover, which in itself affected the appearance only and not the speed of the crew. Such old rowing men as still entertained theories about "professional strokes" engendered by the Yale '82 and '83 crews, were inclined to refer derisively to the style of the '86 crew as a "professional elbow stroke."

The Yale crew had worked all the year with Mr. Robert J. Cook, of Yale '76, as coach. Under Mr. Cook's skillful direction, the men had been taught to apply their power in the same manner as the best professional scullers did. The recover was under excellent control. Although Yale had undoubtedly developed faster crews in subsequent years, it is an interesting fact that for the next twelve years — except for one year that Harvard won, and another year in which all contests between Harvard and Yale had been prohibited by the Harvard authorities — the Yale crews annually defeated the opposing Harvard crews. During all that period Mr. Cook was in charge of the Yale crews and made little or no change in the method of teaching or in the details of the stroke, the recover, especially, of some of them was a model and the despair of their Harvard rivals.

It was especially unfortunate for Harvard to lose this '86 race, as it afforded confirmation of the theory of undergraduate incompetence at a critical time when a victory following the success of the '85 crew might have brought the older and the younger rowing men into an attitude of greater sympathy and mutual understanding. The crew had a feeling that for these two years they had been regarded by the older men as living in sin, the effect of which could only be wiped out by constant victory.

This year the '89 Freshman race was rowed about 11.30 on the morning of the University race, and three crews, representing Harvard, Yale, and Columbia, took part. This was the first of the long series of races for Yale and Harvard Freshman crews. The river was far from smooth and although the three crews were about even at the first half-mile mark, the Harvard crew from that point drew ahead rapidly, winning from Columbia by four boat lengths. The Yale boat filled with water in the first mile and did not finish, the men being picked up by their launch.

Harvard 1886 Crew

G. S. Mumford, '87	(149)	W. A. Brooks, Jr., '87	(166)
Bow		H. W. Keyes, '87	(165)
J. J. Colony, L. S.	(156)	R. F. A. Penrose, Jr., Gr.	(165)
J. R. Yocom, M. S.	(170)	Stroke	
F. Remington, '87	(156)	T. Q. Browne, Jr., '88	(96)
T. P. Burgess, '87	(173)	Coxswain	

Average weight 162½ lbs.

Yale 1886 Crew

R. Appleton, '86	(151)	A. Cowles, Jr., '86	(170)
Bow		C. W. Hartridge, '87	(164)
John Rogers, Jr., '87	(160)	E. L. Caldwell, '87	(147)
J. W. Middlebrook, '87	(163)	Stroke	
F. A. Stevenson, '88	(160)	L. E. Cadwell, '86	(84)
G. W. Woodruff, '89	(169)	Coxswain	

Average weight 159 lbs.

[51]

Columbia 1886 Crew

G. Richards, '87	(155)	S. Harris, '87	(179)
Bow		C. E. Beckwith, '88	(168)
R. C. Applegate, '89	(167)	B. Lockwood, Jr., '87	(159)
C. A. Stevens, '87	(163)	Stroke	
W. A. Meikleham, '86	(168)	R. L. Morrill, '88	(104)
C. M. Donnelly, '87	(175)	Coxswain	

Average weight 167 lbs.

In November, 1886, was celebrated the two hundred and fiftieth anniversary of the founding of Harvard College, and graduates, public men and persons of national prominence, including the President of the United States, Grover Cleveland, flocked to Cambridge from all parts of the country.

A boat race was arranged for November 9th between crews which the *Daily Crimson* fantastically described as representing the best of the graduates and of the undergraduates. In effect the race was between a crew organized by "Foxey" Bancroft, representing the school of rowing which employed the short slide and long body swing, and a crew organized by James J. Storrow from the men of the 1885 crew, with their long slide and shorter body reach. As a matter of fact the test was not very reliable, neither crew being perfectly representative, as Bancroft had only six of his old associates and pupils, the two bow seats being taken by class crew undergraduates, while Storrow's crew had a class crew man for stroke.

The *Crimson* for November 10, 1886, gives the make-up of the crews as follows:

Stroke, W. A. Bancroft '78, the stroke of the '76 to '79 crews; No. 7, F. W. Smith '79, the No. 7 in the '77 to '79 crews; No. 6, F. L. Sawyer '83, of the '81, '82, '83, and '84 crews; No. 5, O. J. Pfeiffer, Medical, of the '81 crew; No. 4, C. P. Curtis, Jr., '83, the stroke of the '81 and '82 crews, and No. 3, E. D. Brandigee '81, of the '80 and '81 crews. Storrow's crew, counting from stroke, consisted of Charles F. Adams '88, James J. Storrow '85, J. J. Colony '85, T. P. Burgess '87, George S. Mumford '87, H. W. Keyes '87, Edward C. Storrow '89, J. R. Yocom '85, bow.

Storrow's eight won the half-mile stretch that was rowed in front of the old boat house by considerably more than a boat length, and at the request of the loser the same trial was immediately made over again, with the same result.

These races really proved nothing except that at any rate rowing standards had not deteriorated since the "good old days."

1887

Yale won by five boat lengths

Henry W. Keyes, class of '87, of Boston, was elected captain of the University crew immediately after the '86 race.

George Faulkner again volunteered his services as coach under the same conditions as before, and they were used for a part of the season by the crew management.

There was some good new material available from the '89 Freshman crew, which defeated the Yale and Columbia Freshmen in the two-mile race the previous June. Edward C. Storrow '89, a cousin of Captain James J. Storrow, Jr., of the '85 University crew, had rowed stroke in the Freshman boat, and was given the same position in the '87 University crew.

During the winter course of training, the captain made no effort to put to work any of the other members of the '86 crew who were still in College, but after the crew got on the river, W. A. Brooks, Jr., who had rowed No. 6 in the '85 and '86 crews, was placed at No. 7.

After the class races Davis '89 and Pfeiffer '89, who had rowed at No. 5 and stroke respectively in the Sophomore boat, were placed in the University crew at Nos. 5 and 6.

The impression prevailed, as a result of the experience of the '86 crew, that a four-mile race against Columbia within one week of the Yale race might frequently prove an injury rather than a help to the chances of winning the Yale race, which was the real objective of the year's work. The College was very anxious to have this crew wipe out, if possible, what it considered the disgrace of the defeat by Columbia in '86 and it was the general expectation that if Harvard should defeat Columbia this year, it would prove the last contest of the kind.

The Columbia crew was made up of nearly the same men that had defeated Harvard the year before, and appeared to row in excellent form. The race was scheduled for one week before the Yale race, but owing to bad weather, postponements took place, so that it was eventually rowed only four days prior to the Harvard–Yale contest.

The race was rowed down stream about 5.30 and neither crew gained a decided lead in the first mile, but in the second mile Harvard having the west course gained about four boat lengths. Columbia regained a little of this subsequently, and in the end was beaten by three boat lengths.

The conditions were fast and Harvard established a new record for the course, of 20 minutes 15 seconds, although some newspapers gave it out as 20 minutes 20 seconds. This record stood for many years as Harvard's best, although Yale beat it in 1888 by five seconds. Columbia's success of the year before had so stimulated interest in the Harvard–Columbia contest that it was considered worth while to run an observation train for a Columbia race. This proved to be the last of the series of Harvard–Columbia four-mile contests.

In the Harvard–Yale race, the same week, the Harvard crew appeared to be in poor condition, showing little of the life and dash that it displayed in the race with Columbia, and Yale had apparently little difficulty in defeating Harvard by a little more margin than Harvard a few days before had beaten Columbia.

[55]

The race was rowed up stream on July 1st at 7.30 in the evening. Harvard had the east and Yale the west course.

In rowing up stream with a favoring tide, especially when the tide is not quite at high, the east crew is favored by faster water at the start, but is in much the slower course in the third mile. The course in those days was absolutely straight and did not follow the channel as it did later.

Both crews rowed about thirty-three strokes to the minute throughout the first half mile and at that flag Harvard led by half a length. In the next half mile Yale passed Harvard and won the race in 22 minutes 56 seconds. Harvard's time was 23 minutes 10 seconds.

The preliminary trials of speed on the part of Harvard, Yale, and Columbia while at New London had given an unusual opportunity for observers to judge of their relative merits, and all the coaches agreed that three more nearly equal crews had never been seen at one time on the river. It has always been thought by the Harvard rowing authorities that if Yale had been a third contestant in the Columbia race, a few days before, the Harvard crew might have defeated both Columbia and Yale.

The Harvard crew cannot be fairly judged by the form it showed in the Yale race, for the boat appeared to drag and the men to row without life all through the last three miles of that contest. In the Columbia race they showed good form, a lot of life, excellent control of the recover and rowed a long stroke, and in this latter respect they were distinctly better than the '86 crew.

Although the rowing season had not been so unsuccessful as that of '86, the College and more especially the crew felt that it had been necessary not only to defeat Yale, but to prove by so doing, that contrary to the prevailing impression, a professional could teach a crew to row in proper form without rushing the recover, and to vindicate also the right of the undergraduate body represented by the captain to keep the management of the crew in its own control.

The '90 Freshman race was rowed the day before the University race with Yale, at 6.30 in the afternoon by Harvard and Columbia. Yale this year did not enter. The race was an easy victory for Columbia. At the first half-mile flag they led Harvard by seven seconds and won the race by nearly seven boat lengths.

Harvard 1887 Crew

A. P. Butler, '88	(158)	E. C. Pfeiffer, '89	(168)
Bow		W. A. Brooks, Jr., '87	(166)
J. W. Wood, Jr., '88	(160)	E. C. Storrow, '89	(140)
H. W. Keyes, '87	(160)	Stroke	
C. E. Schroll, '89	(161)	T. Q. Browne, Jr., '88	(96)
J. T. Davis, '89	(167)	Coxswain	

Average weight 160 lbs.

Yale 1887 Crew

R. M. Wilcox, '88	(146)	F. A. Stevenson, '88	(164)
Bow		G. R. Carter, '88	(158)
C. O. Gill, '89	(161)	E. L. Caldwell, '87	(150)
John Rogers, Jr., '87	(156)	Stroke	
J. W. Middlebrook, '87	(162)	R. Thompson, '90	(104)
G. W. Woodruff, '89	(166)	Coxswain	

Average weight 158 lbs.

[57]

1888

Yale won by twenty-five boat lengths

After their race the feeling of the members of the '87 crew was so unanimous that the result was not a fair measure of the real difference between the Yale and Harvard crews, that at first there was with them an ill-defined desire to try it over again next year with the same men. Captain Keyes and Brooks, No. 7, were graduating, to be sure, but they both professed an intention of returning in the autumn in post-graduate schools, and accordingly no new captain had been elected.

The Athletic Committee, although ignorant of rowing matters, was fired by a praiseworthy desire to help all it could to produce a successful crew. Early in the fall an impression started from somewhere and gradually gained headway, that a desperate rowing situation existed which called for prompt action. The statement was made that there was no system, and with perfect truth it was added that some sort of a system was essential to continued success over a period of years. This movement, if it may be so called, gathered headway and a meeting was held, where it was argued that inasmuch as Captain Keyes had not returned to College, and that there was in fact no actual crew organization in existence, something should be done, and it was decided to recommend the unprecedented step of placing rowing matters completely in the charge of a committee of graduates.

It is certain that the Athletic Committee, the graduates and the undergraduates, all sincerely wanted to bring about but one result, namely, the creation of some system that would ensure the defeat of Yale in the annual race, but the situation was a difficult one. The Yale system under the direction of Cook was proving extremely effective; he had able lieutenants who performed most of the drudgery of coaching, and it looked as if he would bring to the line year after year a series of crews of a very high order. It was all very well to talk about building up a similar system at Harvard, but Harvard had no Cook amongst her graduates. It might be asked why a good professional coach was not employed, and the answer is that eight-oared college rowing was then little understood by professional scullers, and there were really no suitable ones to be had. Faulkner was useful to help out, but he could not possibly have taken charge of a rowing system. It was also a fact that the Harvard authorities shrank from putting professionally coached crews against Yale crews coached by a Yale man, and a former amateur. Too much time and energy was wasted at Harvard in controversies over styles of stroke and whether this or that crew rowed in the right way, while no man or group of men were being developed to build up a permanent system, as had taken place at Yale.

The graduates were divided into camps, all equally keen for victory, but unable to come to any agreement with respect to the amount of responsibility to be put upon the captain. It is probable that the group that supported the proposition that authority should rest primarily with a graduate rowing committee, and which now tried to build a system around this central idea, misjudged the causes for the defeats inflicted by Yale in 1886 and 1887. Although the final results in both years furnished a condemnation of undergraduate management, they failed to recognize how much the Columbia races both years had had to do with the outcome.

The Athletic Committee, acting on the recommendation previously mentioned, appointed a Graduate Rowing Committee consisting of Messrs. R. C. Watson '69, Chairman, Robert Bacon '80, and Francis Peabody, Jr., a Law School graduate of eight years before, together with Captain Keyes of the '87 crew. These men were of course all old Varsity oarsmen.

This rowing committee picked Emil Charles Pfeiffer, Jr. '89, who rowed No. 6 in the '87 crew, for captain.

The rowing committee did not hold a mere advisory position, but was constituted in theory and actually as the executive head of a system which was to restore Harvard's rowing prestige. In practice the fourth member, Keyes, never acted with the others, but remained on his farm in northern New Hampshire, leaving to his three associates the task of running the system, and to Mr. Watson fell the active duties of coach of the University crew.

Mr. Watson soon became actually in his own person the whole committee, for it appeared to be impracticable to divide the responsibility of selecting and coaching the crew.

The rowing men in College supported the new system with absolute loyalty. It was evident that if this system or any other could only prove successful they would be more than satisfied.

Walter Alexander '87, then in the Law School, who had rowed stroke of the winning class crew his Senior year was selected for stroke, and a number of new men were given seats in the boat, of unusual size and power, if indeed they all did not possess skill in proportion.

[60]

R. Clifford Watson, '69, in 1888

Captain Pfeiffer was dismissed by Mr. Watson early in the spring and Edward C. Storrow '89, stroke of the '87 University crew, was appointed captain. Storrow rowed this year at bow.

That this effort of the Athletic Committee to build up a system of Harvard rowing through a graduate rowing committee with autocratic powers was to prove a complete failure became increasingly obvious some time before the day of the race. The crew showed no evidence whatever of speed before leaving for New London, and was easily defeated by other crews in practice on the Charles River.

The Yale race resulted in the most disastrous defeat Harvard has ever suffered. The Yale crew ran away from Harvard as though the latter was anchored. The conditions were exceedingly fast — the winning crew in fact making a record for the course which stood as such for nearly thirty years — and the losing crew was at least one quarter of a mile behind when the winner crossed the finish line. Had the race been against a head wind, a comparison with other racing records shows that Harvard would have been beaten by about three-eighths of a mile. The Harvard crew did not appear to break down, it was simply slow.

The Yale crew was very well together and may have been, and quite possibly was, the fastest crew turned out at New Haven up to that time. The recover was under a control that seemed little short of marvelous. A comparison with the Harvard crew is instructive. The Harvard men emphasized a deep and at the same time a hard catch by a heave with the shoulders, a catch in fact so hard and deep in the water that equal force could not possibly be carried on through the rest of the stroke, and as a result many of the men suffered a jerk of their heads, as they found that the boat failed to respond to such a violent thrust at the water. It is not enough to call it merely a poor crew for it was so slow that Yale rowed away from it from the very first stroke, and the great space that divided the crews at the finish was to all men a true measure of the extent to which the new system had proved to be a failure. The new rowing system was dead, without further formality or ceremony of any kind. The end was due entirely to the defeat by twenty-five boat lengths.

During its brief period of authority the Graduate Rowing Committee had decided to abandon the Columbia race, in which decision it must have been influenced, either consciously or unconsciously, by the true history of the '86 and '87 contests.

This year the first Weld boat house was begun out of a fund presented by George W. Weld, Esq., of Boston.

The time of the Yale crew was 20 minutes and 10 seconds, which remained the record for nearly thirty years.

The Freshman '91 race was rowed at New London over a two-mile course, between Harvard and Columbia Freshman crews and was won without great difficulty by Columbia by four boat lengths. Yale Freshmen this year rowed the Pennsylvania Freshmen.

Harvard 1888 Crew

E. C. Storrow, '89	(145)	E. C. Schroll, '89	(161)
Bow		J. R. Finlay, '91	(190)
J. Markoe, '89	(178)	W. Alexander, L. S.	(154)
P. Trafford, '89	(169)	Stroke	
B. Tilton, '90	(179)	J. E. Whitney, '89	(100)
J. T. Davis, '89	(170)	Coxswain	

Average weight 168 lbs.

Yale 1888 Crew

R. M. Wilcox, '88	(152)	F. A. Stevenson, '88	(168)
Bow		G. R. Carter, '88	(160)
C. O. Gill, '89	(170)	S. M. Cross, '88	(159)
G. S. Brewster, '91	(168)	Stroke	
J. A. Hartwell, '89	(165)	R. Thompson, '90	(106)
W. H. Corbin, '89	(177)	Coxswain	

Average weight 165 lbs.

1889

Yale won by six boat lengths

The season of preparation for the '89 race began with literally no sort of an organization whatever to build on. Captain Edward C. Storrow '89 held over from the year before, but he positively declined to take charge for the new season.

Harvard's attempt to create a rowing system had ended in the overwhelming defeat of the previous season, but that some permanent system was desirable was still believed. Yale had Robert J. Cook and Cornell employed Charles E. Courtney, the famous sculler from Union Springs, New York State. Why could not Harvard provide herself with a Cook or a Courtney? After the 1888 fiasco the impression prevailed that the coach must first be found and the system might then be built up around him, but the Graduate Rowing Committee of the year before had proved to contain among its members no man suitable for such a purpose.

During the six following years a hand-to-mouth policy was pursued. Each captain in succession obtained the services of one or more former Harvard oarsmen to coach his crew, each looking only to success for the crew of his own year. These coaches were all busy men, working either in the Law School or in business, yet it was realized then as well as it is now that a permanent coach was essential if anything better than an occasional victory was to be hoped for. In more recent years a group of men has been gradually formed who had sufficient rowing knowledge, teaching ability, and above all the prestige that success alone can give, to command the confidence of the graduates and undergraduates alike, and their belief in each other and loyal coöperation constitutes in itself the system, such as it is, that now exists. It needs no edicts from the Athletic Committee to give it authority or to obtain for it respectful consideration from the captain. In 1889 there were at least three different factions or groups, but no one of them was able to take hold of our rowing and put it on a permanent and satisfactory basis.

This time the Athletic Committee appeared to judge it best to let the rowing situation slumber. Finally, in the early winter Robert F. Herrick '90, of Boston, who had rowed stroke of his Freshman crew, and had also stroked his Sophomore class crew, which easily won the class races in 1888, was elected captain of the University crew. He selected as coach James J. Storrow '85.

Mr. Storrow, after his successful experience as captain of the '85 University crew, had been in the Harvard Law School, but up to this time, had done practically no active coaching. As a coach, he proved to be exceedingly thorough and painstaking. He worked on the general theory that rowing must be taught to each man individually and that any man who could row well in a single scull or in a pair-oar, if he were physically able to stand the work, would be good material for the University crew.

Interest in rowing was at a low ebb and there was little old material available. With the need of breaking in a lot of new men and little interest being taken in the crew by the undergraduates, together with the prospects of an excellent Yale eight to row against, the problem to be solved seemed unusually difficult.

Throughout the winter the coach held long evening sessions with the candidates, talking over details of the stroke, writing out with infinite care, for their instruction, descriptions of the way the stroke should be rowed, which were studied and discussed.

Captain Herrick took the position of stroke oar, and James P. Hutchinson '90 rowed at No. 7. Neither of these men was a finished oarsman, although they both understood the essentials of fast rowing. They both had an unlimited amount of vigor and energy. Herrick, doubtless owing to his stature, rowed rather stiffly, and proved an exceedingly difficult stroke oar for the rest of the crew to follow.

Six of the seats were filled by men who had had no previous experience in four-mile races until after the class races, when Edward C. Storrow '89, who had stroked the winning Senior class crew, joined the Varsity squad at No. 3. This was his third year in the University boat, bow and No. 2 were taken from their class crews and put in the boat at about the same time.

The race was rowed up stream in the afternoon under fairly favorable conditions. There was the one observation train on the west bank and the usual crowd of small stream craft lined up near the starting point ready to follow the crews. The rival shells had been towed down from their respective quarters, and the Harvard crew had taken possession of a small boat house near the starting line. The Yale eight rowed over leisurely to the line and all eyes watched for the appearance of Harvard. After half an hour had elapsed the referee notified Harvard's official representative that Harvard must immediately come out or Yale would be sent over the course alone. The Yale official, rather than have this happen, preferred to wait a little longer. After a further interval that seemed like hours to the impatient spectators, the referee declared that Yale must proceed without Harvard, whereupon luckily the Harvard shell put in its appearance.

The delay had been caused by certain last touches or changes to the rigging and braces of the shell, doubtless of some value in themselves, but was much more than counterbalanced by the strain that the long wait had on the men.

They could hardly know how nearly they had come to being left out of the race altogether, but their fear of such a possibility and consequent nervousness had become very acute. They appeared hurried and excited, an unfavorable state of mind under which to start the race.

Possibly the impression that the crew was laboring under an unusual nervous strain was also due in part to the fact that they began with a false start, for after this long period of waiting when the crews had been sent off by the referee, they were not allowed to proceed very far up the course before the referee recalled them. It appeared that No. 5 in the Harvard boat had jumped his slide and signaled to the referee for a new start. In this false start the Harvard crew did better than Yale and was leading the opposing crew at the time the referee recalled them. The next time they started Yale at once took the lead and kept it.

The two crews were not very uneven and the handicap under which Harvard labored as a result of this delay may have contributed somewhat to the extent of her defeat. Yale soon had a good lead which she gradually increased, defeating Harvard by five or six boat lengths in 21 minutes and 39 seconds.

This Yale crew probably was not fast and it was remarked at the time that it was Harvard's chance to win if she was ever going to win a race from Yale. Neither crew seemed to be "well to-gether" but Harvard had a noticeable hang or wasted motion at the full reach, some of the oar blades being carried high off the water at that point in the stroke.

This fault of clipping or carrying the blade high just before the beginning of the stroke was a characteristic fault of other Har-vard crews besides this one. In this respect the Yale crews pre-sented a marked contrast. Yale coaches with reason took pride in their success in teaching their crews to carry their oar blades close to the water just before the beginning of the stroke, which undoubtedly accounted in part for the fact that Yale crews ap-peared to row a longer stroke than Harvard.

This was the only University crew for which James J. Storrow, Jr., ever acted as coach, but his advice was frequently sought in subsequent years in connection with the work of many later crews.

Several of the men who rowed between 1885 and 1889 con-tinued after graduation to take an active personal interest, most of these have actually coached later University crews, and they have all held an important place in Harvard rowing history. James J. Storrow '85, George S. Mumford '87, and Henry W. Keyes '87 rowed in the crew of 1885, and the two latter in sub-sequent crews. Edward C. Storrow '89 stroked the 1887 crew and rowed in the crews of the two following years. Charles F. Adams '88 was a substitute for the '86 crew, while Robert F. Herrick '90 and James P. Hutchinson '90 were respectively stroke and No. 7 of the '89 crew, and Hutchinson stroked the '90 University crew. Thomas Nelson Perkins '91 rowed No. 2 in the '89 crew, and on two succeeding crews. Harvard rowing for the past thirty-five years has been considerably influenced by all of these men in varying degree.

The race between the Freshman crews of the class of '92 was won by Harvard over Columbia by a couple of boat lengths. This two-mile race was again rowed without Yale as a participant, the latter rowing the Pennsylvania Freshmen instead.

Harvard 1889 Crew

G. PERRY, '89	(163)	B. T. TILTON, '90	(185)
Bow		J. P. HUTCHINSON, '90	(157)
T. N. PERKINS, '91	(162)	R. F. HERRICK, '90	(156)
E. C. STORROW, '89	(147)	Stroke	
J. S. CRANSTON, '91	(184)	J. E. WHITNEY, '89	(106)
J. R. FINLAY, '91	(188)	Coxswain	

Average weight 168 lbs.

Yale 1889 Crew

C. F. ROGERS, '90	(160)	G. W. WOODRUFF, '89	(176)
Bow		P. ALLEN, '90	(161)
C. O. GILL, '89	(176)	E. L. CALDWELL, T. S.	(153)
G. S. BREWSTER, '91	(171)	Stroke	
J. A. HARTWELL, '89	(170)	R. THOMPSON, '90	(113)
W. H. CORBIN, '89	(178)	Coxswain	

Average weight 168 lbs.

1890

Yale won by three boat lengths

Benjamin T. Tilton, class of '90, was elected captain after the race. He resigned early in the autumn and Robert F. Herrick, class of 1890, was again chosen captain of the crew.

The members of the '89 crew were much discouraged over their defeat, as they had had great confidence in James J. Storrow, their coach, and felt that if he had been unable to overcome Mr. Cook, they did not know who could.

Herrick, with the help of Henry W. Keyes '87, guided the preliminary work, but before the season was far advanced he announced to the crew squad that he doubted the wisdom of his rowing on the crew and insisted upon resigning his position as captain.

The men elected James P. Hutchinson of Philadelphia, class of 1890, captain of the crew.

Hutchinson directed the work personally. It can be hardly said that he formally selected any one as regular coach of the crew, although several men did more or less coaching, but he did depend on Mr. Keyes as his chief and constant adviser.

Henry W. Keyes was the captain of the 1887 University crew, and had coached the '91 Freshmen two years before this at New London. He had rowed in the '85, '86, and '87 Yale races and understood perfectly what were the essentials to success in college rowing. As a teacher his experience had heretofore been limited, but he proved to be an excellent coach, and for four years was

Henry W. Keyes, '87, in his Senior Year

looked upon by the crews and the College as the nominal if not always the actual head of our organization.

As he ran a stock farm in northern New Hampshire, it was taken for granted that he could be master of his own time, and would in fact make the development of the crews figure as his chief business for a part of each year, for some time to come. As a matter of fact Keyes when amongst his bulls and calves found the occupation too engrossing to admit of any other distraction after this year except for an occasional visit to Cambridge and a longer stay in New London, and he doubtless at this time laid plans for the subsequent political career that has eventually carried him into the United States Senate.

He did devote a lot of time to the '90 University crew, and spent perhaps three entire weeks at the end of the season with the '91 crew, but thereafter he found little further time to spare for this work, and seldom quitted his New Hampshire farm.

The effort to find a suitable man to row stroke occupied much of the attention of Captain Hutchinson throughout the early season. In the end he decided to take that position himself, but as he had never rowed on the port side and believed that he never could learn to be as effective on that side as on the starboard, the rigging of the boat had to be changed over to provide for a starboard stroke. With the boat thus rigged, with the even numbers on the starboard side and the odd on the port, Captain Hutchinson assumed the stroke seat.

After the class races Nelson and Kelton were taken out of the Freshman boat and put in at bow and No. 6 respectively. It was a strong tough crew, but never succeeded in getting well together, and had poor control of the recover.

[71]

Its fighting spirit was unusually good, and although on the whole composed of excellent material, it was Hutchinson's personality that really gave it its peculiar characteristic. It would be most unfair to say of it that if it could not row, at least it could fight, for it not only did row well enough to have won with only a slight turn of better luck, but it was the kind of crew that was not beaten until the finish line was crossed. It was a dangerous crew for any rival to treat with contempt, merely because it did not look as smooth and machine-like as some. Hutchinson was determined that it should not lose because of too little work, and in the last three or four weeks he drove it almost daily over the four miles, and for a wonder the crew did not seem to suffer under the experience and entered the race in excellent condition.

The Harvard and Yale crews of the '80's and the first half of the '90's regarded each other with unfriendly eyes. In fact the wonder is that with such strong feeling towards each other as then existed, the break did not occur earlier than came about in 1895 between the colleges over football. As a body, each camp entirely distrusted the other, but it is only fair to say that the Harvard men regarded the individual Yale men, with the exception of Mr. Cook, as reasonable and sane beings like themselves, and the Yale men doubtless reciprocated. Mr. Cook personally was unconciliatory and certainly he did not always make himself agreeable to or inspire affection in the breasts of the Harvard men. After a great many years of negotiations and discussions with successive Harvard captains over various matters connected with arrangements for the races, some important and some trifling, he had created a sort of boyish tradition that unless Harvard kept herself very much alive, even before the race was rowed she was almost as good as beaten through Mr. Cook's ingenuity in profiting by her mistake, or through some oversight on the Harvard captain's part.

It was then supposed that a merit existed in hiding from their rivals their own time records and detecting in turn the time records of the enemy. This duty fell to the substitutes, and originated doubtless in the need of finding some occupation for these unfortunates. The chasm between them and a member of the eight was very great, and in no respect was this more marked than in the amount of rowing they accomplished each day. The easiest way to get real work out of the two substitutes was for the captain to direct them to row down the course three miles, and wait at that point to catch the time of the last mile of the rival crew should it chance to go over the full four miles later in the day. The labor of rowing down three miles and back again in a heavy pair-oar was by no means slight. The general effect was that of enemy outposts established to spy on each other. A blue or a red jersey might be detected lurking behind some friendly tree or rock anywhere along the course, whenever one or the other crew might be expected to come along. This constant appearance of secret watching always annoyed and sometimes enraged the enemy.

The race was rowed down stream, Harvard having the west course. At the start the Harvard crew was thought to have jumped into the lead, but if so, Yale almost immediately forged ahead, and the two crews raced down the first mile side by side, each making alternate spurts, but Yale always somewhat in the lead. This continued until they had passed the mile-and-one-half flag and it seemed clear that at last the rivals were having a real race. During the next mile the Harvard boat rolled down on

[73]

one side, probably due to poor watermanship on some man's part, and Yale began to draw ahead. Harvard was apparently struggling at this point and lost her stride. At the two-and-one-half-mile flag Yale had extended her lead to about two lengths of open water and from there on found it impossible to make any further gain. The Harvard boat from this point, having recovered its balance, and the men rowing very hard and with extraordinary life and vigor, held Yale until the finish was reached.

The Yale recover seemed much better than Harvard's, the effect being, as usual with two such crews in a race, that the Harvard men pushed their boat further on each stroke, but lost more during the recover than Yale.

The time of the Yale crew was 21 minutes 29 seconds, and Harvard 21 minutes 40 seconds.

On the whole the closeness of the race was a surprise, as the newspapers had led the public to believe that Yale had an unusually fast crew and that the Harvard crew was poor.

This was the fifth successive race that Yale had won and it seemed as if Harvard was never again to win a race.

It has been said that this was a critical year in Harvard rowing history and that if we had won we might have been saved some of the ensuing years of defeat. We did win the next year, and it is not quite clear that an extra victory in 1890 would have done anything more towards establishing our much desired system. James J. Storrow and Keyes were the only possible men to do it, and neither would give the necessary time. One of them might coach this crew and the other that, but only an occasional victory seemed to be at all likely.

The Freshman race was still contested with Columbia, and

the Harvard and Columbia crews of the class of '93 rowed their race at New London on the same day as the University race.

Harvard had some promising material in her boat, but the race was won by Columbia in a very close finish by a couple of seconds, the distance between the crews being half a boat's length.

In the eleven years in which these annual Freshman contests had been held Harvard had won six times and Columbia five. Yale Freshmen were this year defeated by the Cornell Freshman crew.

Harvard 1890 Crew

G. L. Nelson, '93	(159)	G. H. Kelton, '93	(190)
Bow		B. T. Tilton, '90	(187)
F. Winthrop, '91	(160)	J. P. Hutchinson, '90	(152)
J. H. Goddard, '92	(174)	Stroke	
T. N. Perkins, '91	(159)	H. M. Battelle, '93	(100)
R. D. Upham, '90	(183)	Coxswain	

Average weight 171 lbs.

Yale 1890 Crew

C. F. Rogers, '90	(157)	H. T. Ferris, '91	(184)
Bow		S. B. Ives, '93	(168)
W. A. Simms, '90	(163)	P. Allen, '90	(159)
G. S. Brewster, '91	(183)	Stroke	
J. A. Hartwell, P. G.	(169)	R. Thompson, '90	(117)
A. B. Newell, '90	(183)	Coxswain	

Average weight 171 lbs.

1891

Harvard won by eleven boat lengths

Thomas Nelson Perkins of Milton, Massachusetts, class of '91, was elected captain of the crew after the '90 race.

Tilton and Hutchinson, who rowed No. 7 and stroke, were the only members of that crew who had graduated.

Captain Perkins took charge of the work of the crew, as had Captain Hutchinson the year before, and Mr. Charles F. Adams '88 did most of the preliminary coaching. Mr. Adams had been a substitute for the crew of 1886. Both he and Perkins had great confidence in the value of Keyes' help, when they could get it. Early in the season Captain Perkins on the advice of a majority of former captains, called together to discuss the question of coach, had requested the Athletic Committee to appoint Mr. W. A. Bancroft '78 coach of the crew at a fixed salary, for three years. The Athletic Committee declined to do this, but the discussion this affair provoked led to a more general feeling that the paying of a coach was a proper and perhaps necessary proceeding. It also put on record the justice of allowing a new coach more than one year to prove his ability to turn out a winning crew.

As the crew was originally made up Perkins took the position of stroke, with Kelton the only other man from the '90 University crew rowing at No. 7. The rest of the eight were new men.

Perkins proved to be an excellent captain and the crew made good progress. The material was above the average, and, moreover, the captain had succeeded in restoring the old interest and enthusiasm in the College for its crew which had been lacking in several former years. He rowed at stroke himself and inspired the same fighting spirit characteristic of the crew of the previous year, while its rowing form was considerably better.

About June 1st Perkins injured his arm, getting water on the elbow, and the sensation and discouragement throughout the College which followed, almost exactly paralleled that of eight years before, when Charles P. Curtis, Jr. '83, the then stroke, had been forced to give up rowing because of injury to his hip.

John Craig Powers '92, who had been rowing at No. 2 was put at stroke in Captain Perkins' place.

When the crew went to New London the feeling was one of general discouragement. Mr. Keyes assumed the duties of active coach about a week before the men left Cambridge, and remained with them constantly until the race. The crew did not make immediate progress, but about two weeks before the race Perkins went back in the boat at No. 2 and it was then or only shortly before that signs appeared that it was getting together. Powers was proving to be a good smooth-rowing stroke, and, while not very long in the water, he had a lot of driving power and a good control of the recover. The crew in the last two weeks came very rapidly and seldom has a Harvard crew developed as good form and speed during so short a time before the race.

The chief resort for spectators on the night before the race was the Piquot House, located on the west side of the Thames River near its mouth. The two annual events which seemed to justify the existence of this hotel were the Harvard–Yale boat race and the annual cruise of the New York Yacht Club. From these two occasions the gleanings must have sufficed to support the owners for the balance of the year. The sisters and female cousins of the men on the crews disported themselves through the evening in the parlors with such part of the assembled Harvard men, graduates and undergraduates, as from time to time gave over the attractions of the bar in order to waltz. No whiskey was ever seen in that back shed called the bar. A brand of gin was the only liquor, always combined with lemon and sugar and soda water. Recollections of the Piquot House are still chiefly associated with this mixture. Very little sleep was expected. This year every one was on deck early, for the race was to be rowed in the morning.

On the evening before, some Harvard man whose opinion had much weight stated that Yale was going to lose. After our five successive defeats this statement struck most Harvard men as an exaggeration. It was, however, said that Harvard had "got together" and then came real hope, for if it was true, of course there was a chance. If Captain Hutchinson's crew the year before had only "got together" even for a couple of days before the race, it would perhaps have won.

The number of spectators who were Harvard and Yale graduates and undergraduates and members of their families, had steadily increased year by year, and all these expected to be provided with accommodations for viewing the race from start to finish. The only observation was on the west bank, and there was a large fleet of every kind of available river craft which were fast enough to keep up with the crews, especially tug boats, chartered for the race. When the race was rowed down stream all these boats could not possibly find room in the narrow channel opposite the start, and they would place themselves at various

HARVARD UNIVERSITY CREW, '91, AT NEW LONDON

Harvard launch in background

Powers at stroke was doing excellent work. He had started out with a rather high stroke, and when his crew obtained a good lead did not let it down appreciably, but continued to drive the crew, and it looked as though the whole eight wanted to beat Yale as thoroughly as possible, to make up for the past five years. Little more was added to the lead in the third mile, but thereafter Harvard added about four more lengths, defeating Yale in all by eleven lengths in 21 minutes and 21 seconds. Yale's time was 21 minutes 57 seconds.

The Yale crew never appeared to get going, and was simply rowed off its balance at the start.

The result was a satisfactory proof of the excellent work done by Captain Perkins, and Keyes deserved great credit for his ability to put speed into the crew in the three or four weeks he had it in charge.

Doctor William M. Conant '79, of Boston, was on hand at New London and assisted the management with advice as to the training and condition of the men. This was significant in view of the defects in the physical condition of the men in other years.

After this victory, when reading in the newspapers the usual advice as to the way the crews should row, it was a relief to note for a change that this wisdom was all to the effect that Yale and not Harvard rowed what the writers were pleased to call the wrong stroke, and the hope was expressed that the Yale crew would now see the error of their ways in departing from the principles of the regular "Yale stroke" and would return again to correct teachings of former years. It was always with the newspapers that a defeated crew rowed a wrong stroke and never that it executed badly the right stroke.

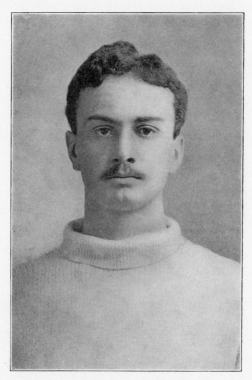

THOMAS NELSON PERKINS, '91,
IN HIS SENIOR YEAR

It is of this race that the anecdote is recorded, that some enthusiastic Harvard supporters following the race in a tug boat lost one of their number overboard near the two-mile flag. The helmsman at once started to turn back to rescue the swimmer, but was prevented from carrying out his purpose by loud shouts to go ahead, "Let him go, it serves him right, we can't stop now." The unfortunate one was picked up by another boat.

The Freshman '94 crews rowed on June 24th, two days before the University race. This time Yale once more took part with Harvard and Columbia. The result was an easy victory for Columbia, which defeated Yale Freshmen by four boat lengths, with Harvard third at the finish. Columbia's time, 9 minutes 41 seconds, was a new record for the two miles.

Harvard 1891 Crew

M. Newell, '93	(166)	D. R. Vail, '93	(180)
Bow		G. H. Kelton, '93	(193)
T. N. Perkins, '91	(164)	J. C. Powers, '92	(159)
N. Rantoul, '92	(167)	Stroke	
F. Lynam, M. S.	(168)	H. M. Battelle, '93	(100)
C. K. Cummings, '93	(181)	Coxswain	

Average weight 172 lbs.

Yale 1891 Crew

W. A. Simms, M. S.	(163)	G. S. Brewster, '91	(176)
Bow		P. Hagerman, L. S.	(174)
A. J. Balliet, '92	(164)	J. A. Gould, '92	(164)
C. R. Ely, '91	(166)	Stroke	
R. D. Paine, '94	(183)	H. S. Brown, '93	(110)
W. W. Hefflefinger, '91	(200)	Coxswain	

Average weight 174 lbs.

1892

Yale won by twenty boat lengths

Thomas Nelson Perkins, class of '91, had been reëlected captain after the '91 race. He entered the Law School the following season, but resigned as soon as College opened, having decided not to row because of his injured elbow, and George H. Kelton '93 was elected in his place. Practically all of the '91 crew were still in College, but the rosy prospects faded away for one reason after another.

The first great loss was that of Perkins, the captain. Then came that of Powers, who had proved himself to be a good stroke. Powers decided not to row.

Two big men, Acton and Waters, were discovered and placed in the waist of the boat, which proved to be a mistake as neither of them learned to row, and a very big man, who has not worked in with the others, always bothers a crew more than would a man of average size.

The one real interesting feature about this rowing season was the Yale crew itself.

Since the defeat of Yale in 1885 Robert J. Cook had devoted an extraordinary amount of intelligent effort to Yale rowing. His rowing career began before the time of sliding seats and before eight-oared shells came into use in this country. He rowed for five successive years on Yale crews against Harvard, from 1872 to 1876 inclusive, and the last four at stroke. He was chiefly instrumental in organizing the Harvard–Yale four-mile eight-oared races, and was himself stroke of the original Yale eight in the first of these contests in 1876. This was the race in which Foxey Bancroft of Harvard '78 rowed at stroke for the first time, and suffered his only defeat by a Yale University crew.

Mr. Cook was a man of unusual determination and physical vigor, as is well illustrated by an incident during the season of 1886. A negro janitor in his office in Philadelphia attacked him unawares with an axe and drove the blade into Cook's skull. After disposing of his assailant, Mr. Cook walked to the hospital and had a large piece of bone removed from the top of his head. His life was saved with difficulty, but in a short time he was back working over the '86 crew harder than ever.

By the end of another year Cook had developed several younger coaches, trained in his methods, who took off from his shoulders the burden of teaching the rudiments to individual men. It was a frequent experience for a Harvard man visiting Philadelphia and taking his dinner at the famous old Hotel Bellevue to observe Mr. Cook throughout the entire evening conferring with rowing men from New Haven, who came to consult the oracle almost daily. He would give up the entire month of June to New London and the crew. His authority was based on his success, and the support of a large and influential body of Yale graduates. Bulldog determination, intelligence, and knowledge were his assets, and with them he largely dominated the Harvard–Yale rowing situation for nearly twenty-five years.

And now after almost a defeat in 1890 and a real disaster in 1891 he developed a crew with the valuable help of Captain Hartwell, who had also rowed in the very fast 1888 crew, which proved to be probably the fastest of them all, perhaps the fastest that Yale has ever had. It seemed as if no crew could be more perfectly together or row more smoothly, and it also had plenty of power, of that there can be no doubt. It must have been great fun to be one of these eight men, and form a part of that perfect machine. As between such a crew and the Harvard crew, there could not be a real race.

It is only fair to say that the distance between two rival crews at the end of a four-mile contest is not always an exact measure of their relative speed. For instance, in 1908 Harvard beat Yale by half a mile, but the crews were so nearly even at the two-mile flag that it was impossible to hazard any guess then as to which would win. In that year they fought each other like two bulls with locked horns until one or the other weakened.

In the '92 race the Yale crew darted off so fast that clear water showed between Yale's stern and the bow of the Harvard shell in less than a dozen strokes, and there was nothing after that to cause either crew to collapse from actual racing strain.

Crews cannot race with much enthusiasm after it is clearly realized what the result is going to be. A few extra boat lengths added on at the end to a long gap already made between the boats gives little more glory to the winner, and a cutting down of the space by one or two boat lengths by frantic exertion after the race is practically over certainly affords even less of solace to the hopelessly defeated crew.

The result of this race was settled as soon as it began. This is not meant as a criticism of the spirit and character of the men in the Harvard boat, they were a very fine set of men, but the simple fact was that they never got into any sort of a stride during the race, and struggled on without hope for those long four miles.

The race was rowed down stream on July 1st under fast conditions, and was an exact reversal of the year before. This time it was Yale that jumped right to the front and it was Harvard that floundered and failed to get going.

Yale rowed the four miles in 20 minutes and 48 seconds. Harvard's time was 21 minutes and 42 seconds. Under the conditions which prevailed that afternoon, this was equivalent to about twenty boat lengths.

The Freshman race for the class of '95 was rowed the same day between Harvard, Yale, and Columbia. Harvard had a poor crew and came in third, about twenty-five seconds behind Yale, who won. Columbia was also slow enough, and Yale beat her by nearly twenty seconds in the two miles.

Harvard 1892 Crew

M. Newell, '93	(173)	F. Winthrop, L. S.	(165)
Bow		G. H. Kelton, '93	(194)
N. Rantoul, '92	(167)	F. Lynam, M. S.	(172)
B. G. Waters, '94	(188)	Stroke	
R. Acton, M. S.	(195)	V. Thomas, '95	(105)
C. K. Cummings, '93	(188)	Coxswain	

Average weight 180 lbs.

Yale 1892 Crew

F. A. Johnson, '94	(160)	J. A. Hartwell, M. S.	(170)
Bow		S. B. Ives, '93	(172)
A. J. Balliet, '92	(165)	E. F. Gallaudet, '93	(172)
A. L. Van Huyck, '93	(170)	Stroke	
R. D. Paine, '94	(192)	F. E. Olmstead, '94	(105)
A. B. Graves, '92	(167)	Coxswain	

Average weight 171 lbs.

1893

Yale won by three and a half boat lengths

Davis R. Vail, class of '93, who rowed No. 6 in the '91 University crew, was captain of this crew.

In these days the crews used both the tank and rowing machines for the winter work. The tank had always been more of an institution with Yale crews than with Harvard, and some coach at New Haven under Mr. Cook had advised a method of using it to teach the recover and the catch so successfully that Harvard crews could never equal their rivals in these respects. It was said that it was the practice in the tank that did it. Perhaps it was, but if so, Harvard's coaches did not understand the tank, for Harvard's superiority over Yale when it did exist was always in drive and dash, which certainly could not be learned in the tank, where about ten strokes to the minute was the most that could be rowed.

There were a lot of old men back in College and the material was very fair.

The three men whose names are associated with the coaching of the crews from 1890 to 1894 inclusive are Henry W. Keyes '87, Charles F. Adams, 2d '88, and Thomas Nelson Perkins '91. Mr. Keyes' fame rests chiefly on his achievement with the '91 crew, which defeated Yale so satisfactorily and thoroughly, but Mr. Adams did practically all the work in the early season and enjoyed with justice not a little of the credit for the victory. Perkins, the captain of the same crew, had done his work as captain well and triumphantly, and the prestige thus deservedly acquired gave him much influence with subsequent crews.

After the '91 race Keyes furnished chiefly the magic of his name to conjure with, and confined his attention strictly to the duties of his farm, but the legend was constantly repeated and believed for the next three years, that when the crews left for New London, he would forthwith put in his appearance and repeat the great work of 1891.

Perkins did most of the work of coaching this year, although Keyes was on hand for a time at New London. Adams did very little actual coaching after 1892.

The man selected for stroke was Edward H. Fennessy '96, a Freshman, who had had some previous rowing experience at St. Paul's School. Cummings '93, who had rowed in the '91 and '92 University crews, rowed No. 7. Vail, the captain, rowed No. 6 and Fearing '93, an entirely new man, at No. 5. He was a good natural athlete, but had a lot to learn during his short experience as an oarsman. The crew as a whole was a little rough, but powerful, and before the race had very nearly succeeded in getting together.

The men at the Harvard quarters were quite confident of success, while the Yale management was not entirely satisfied with its crew or its chances. A few days before the race Mr. Cook removed Ralph D. Paine from the boat. Paine, the same man who later achieved fame as a writer, was much the largest and heaviest man in the boat, and this last-minute change made a lot of talk at the time. He had rowed in two former Harvard races and was popularly supposed to be a first-rate oarsman. In those days such a radical step as taking out one of the four stern men in the last week was so unusual, and for Cook such an unprecedented proceeding as to amount practically to a notice to all the world that he did not think very highly of his crew.

There is no doubt that this was by no means one of Yale's fast crews.

The race was rowed down stream on June 30th against quite a strong head wind. Harvard had the east course and, therefore, was in the poorer position during the second mile. Both crews got off well and Harvard with a fairly high stroke gained a slight lead, which she maintained for nearly one and a half miles. The crews were nearly side by side for this distance and then Yale began to draw ahead.

As long as these races were rowed on a straight line, if the two crews were of exactly equal speed, the crew on the east course was absolutely sure to be passed in the second mile, unless the race was rowed on full high tide or against the tide, but this last never did happen. The reason was that for nearly half a mile the west crew was absolutely in the channel while its rival at the same time was wholly in shallow water with little favoring current.

A spectator watching the two crews on this occasion could observe that Yale at the mile and a half came up and passed Harvard and that Harvard at the same time appeared to lose its stride. It is impossible to say which was cause and which effect, but the probability was that Yale did this because of her advantage of position, and that it rattled the Harvard men to see her suddenly rush past them.

Harvard struggled on after this with little of the form shown earlier in the race, and Yale with an assured lead was able to lengthen out her stroke and row on to the end with perfect confidence.

Yale's time was 25 minutes 1½ seconds and Harvard's, 25 minutes 15 seconds. Under the slow conditions, with a head wind, Harvard appeared to hold Yale surprisingly well in the last part of the race.

The Freshman '96 race was rowed two days before the University race, between Harvard, Yale, and Columbia. Yale came in about seven lengths ahead of Harvard and Columbia was a bad third. Several men on the Harvard Freshman squad figured in subsequent University crews and the class of '96 was the prominent rowing class of its time.

Harvard 1893 Crew

G. E. Burgess, '93	(157)	D. R. Vail, '93	(188)
Bow		C. K. Cummings, '93	(182)
W. S. Johnson, '94	(165)	E. H. Fennessy, '96	(164)
M. Newell, '94	(174)	Stroke	
L. Davis, '94	(179)	V. Thomas, '95	(108)
G. R. Fearing, '93	(173)	Coxswain	

Average weight 173 lbs.

Yale 1893 Crew

F. A. Johnson, '96	(164)	A. P. Rogers, '94	(164)
Bow		S. B. Ives, '94	(174)
E. L. Messler, '94	(174)	E. F. Gallaudet, '93	(174)
A. L. Van Huyck, '94	(171)	Stroke	
J. M. Longacre, '96	(173)	F. E. Olmstead, '94	(106)
J. M. Goetchius, '96	(170)	Coxswain	

Average weight 170½ lbs.

1894

Yale won by seventeen boat lengths

Lincoln Davis, of Boston, class of '94, was elected captain of the crew.

Captain Davis promptly began to plan out the season's work carefully and under the best advice obtainable. He consulted constantly with Mr. Thomas Nelson Perkins, who was still in the Law School, he talked with Mr. W. A. Bancroft '78 and other former coaches and captains, and at Mr. Perkins' suggestion even sent for Courtney, the Cornell coach, with a view to the possibility of engaging him as Harvard's regular coach.

Courtney had been a famous single sculler twenty years before, and had later taken up the coaching of eight-oared crews at Cornell University. At this time he was already known as the very best of professional coaches, and had developed some fast Cornell crews. It was the very next season's Cornell University crew, that of 1895, that he took to England for the Henley Regatta. Courtney spent a week or two with Captain Davis in Cambridge and might have become the coach, had our Athletic Committee consented, and if the Cornell rowing authorities had not decided they had no intention of losing him.

In the end Mr. Perkins gave what time he could to coaching the crew and Mr. Keyes also appeared occasionally.

In spite of every effort to get out the right kind of material, the general lack of interest throughout the College and the failure for one reason and another of the more promising candidates to come up to expectations, made the season's work extremely discouraging. Fennessy, who, as a Freshman, had stroked the crew the year before, rowed stroke, and the rest of the crew, with the exception of the captain, consisted of new material, largely from the Sophomore class.

The conditions under which the crews were selected and trained were still the same as ten and fifteen years before. The University squad was made up of men left over from the previous year's crew, together with the most promising men in the last year's Freshman crew. Two or three new men were hunted up and tried out, but seldom more than a single one now and then ever gained a seat in the boat. In all only eight men formed the squad up to the time of the class races.

The class races were by all odds the most important athletic contests inside the College, and the interest each class took in its own crew, and the rivalry between the crews themselves, was always keen. The University eight plodded along independently of these other four crews, and when their race was over a few of the most likely men in the class crews were added to the University squad, to be taken to New London as substitutes and perhaps to replace one or more of the men who had been rowing heretofore in the eight.

The class races were held May 6th and were won by '96. It was apparent as the result of a trial race, that this Sophomore crew was considerably faster than the University crew, and the management almost decided to take it over bodily as the University crew, and prepare it for the Yale race. The final decision was to take three of the men into the Varsity boat, which made in all six from the Sophomore class out of the eight men making up the crew. A. M. Kales, the Sophomore crew stroke, was placed at stroke in the University boat, Fennessy changing over to the starboard side, to row at No. 7, and Captain Davis rowed No. 6.

This crew never made satisfactory progress and came to the race with little confidence and unsupported by any enthusiasm from the College.

The race was rowed down stream on June 29th. There appeared to be no prospect of any wind, so the Harvard crew removed the washboards from the shell, but before the race started a breeze sprang up, so that the race was rowed in a choppy sea, against a head wind and the Harvard boat took in a lot of water before it was over.

The Yale crew was probably much better than in 1893.

The start was badly handled by the referee, who gave the word while the men in the Harvard boat were disposing of their jerseys, and Yale rowed off leaving its rival struggling to get the boat under way. Instead of recalling them, the referee watched the Yale crew with much apparent interest and doubtless thought, if he thought about it at all, that the result would be just the same, no matter what kind of a start they had.

Harvard did not appear to be in the same class with Yale. The men were determined to do their best and completely exhausted themselves struggling on down the course astern of that Yale crew. The conditions were poor and Yale's time for the four miles was 23 minutes 47 seconds, Harvard's 24 minutes 40 seconds.

There appeared in the newspapers after the race the usual words of advice to Harvard as the loser, to abandon false standards of rowing, and of warning that she would continue to be defeated regularly unless her crews consented to row as Mr. Cook of Yale and Mr. Watson of Harvard believe crews should row. The following is quoted *verbatim*: "Unfortunately very few of the present undergraduates know anything about rowing. There is hardly a man at Harvard who has even seen six boat races in his life . . . . There are more than a dozen graduates in and about Boston who can teach the right stroke, etc." Ever since the defeat of the '86 crew this kind of comment had been annually repeated except in 1888 when the graduates were in charge, and in 1891 when Harvard won. With the '94 race the theory of undergraduate incompetence seemed to be completely established.

In the Freshman race, rowed on the same day as the Varsity, Harvard, Yale, and Columbia '97 took part. The Yale crew won, defeating Columbia by six boat lengths, and Harvard came in a poor third twelve boat lengths behind the winner.

Harvard 1894 Crew

J. Purdon, '95	(157)	L. Davis, '94	(172)
Bow		E. H. Fennessy, '96	(163)
J. R. Bullard, '96	(155)	A. M. Kales, '96	(145)
K. H. Lewis, '96	(165)	Stroke	
R. M. Townsend, '96	(162)	E. B. Day, '96	(100)
T. G. Stevenson, '96	(166)	Coxswain	

Average weight 162 lbs.

Yale 1894 Crew

R. ARMSTRONG, '95	(156)	W. R. CROSS, '96	(195)
Bow		R. B. TREADWAY, '96	(175)
H. C. HOLCOMB, '95	(173)	F. A. JOHNSON, '94	(165)
W. M. BEARD, '96	(179)	Stroke	
A. P. ROGERS, '94	(164)	F. E. OLMSTEAD, '94	(106)
A. W. DATER, '95	(185)	Coxswain	

Average weight 174 lbs.

1895

Yale won by eleven boat lengths

Edward H. Fennessy, of Newton, Massachusetts, was elected Captain of the University crew of 1895.

The Athletic Committee believed itself justified in taking control of the rowing situation.

The method adopted and the course of events was somewhat as follows: Captain Fennessy was advised by some old rowing men and other graduates in whom he had confidence that a coach must be selected who could continue in charge for more than one year. That Colonel Bancroft '78 would be an ideal man, but that while he might have been available four years before, that now he would not consent. That Mr. R. C. Watson '69 was really the only suitable man who could take the position. That because Colonel Bancroft, when the matter had previously been discussed with him, had felt unable to give up the necessary time from his profession except on a three-year contract at a fixed salary, it would be proper and necessary to make with Mr. Watson a three-year contract also, but with this difference that Mr. Watson should receive no pay. A special point also dwelt upon was that Mr. Watson might not win the first year, but for that reason should not be set aside by the next captain, but must be allowed to keep on long enough to afford a fair chance to establish our rowing on a good basis. Captain Fennessy formally requested the Athletic Committee to contract with Mr. Watson on these terms and his request was at once complied with.

It seemed to have occurred to no one at the time that such a contract without any consideration given or received — to use a legal phrase — was very different from an agreement to pay a fixed sum for three years. In the latter case if the boat club decided to dispense with and discontinue the coach's services before the end of the term, a payment of the sum of money due could cancel any further obligation. But in Mr. Watson's case the contract became a sort of moral obligation on both sides for continuing the engagement by an absolute mutual agreement to that effect.

When Mr. Watson began his period of control he felt very strongly the importance of creating both in the college and in the minds of the crew candidates an appreciation of the very strong feeling existing amongst the graduates that our rowing must be more successful, and almost immediately an opportunity presented itself to show that he meant business. For some breach of ethics in their training on the part of the crew candidates, he dismissed Fennessy from his position as captain and directed that Bullard be elected in his place.

John Richards Bullard, of Dedham, Massachusetts, class of '96, served as captain for the next two seasons.

Up to the end of the nineties a constant discussion went on about what was called different kinds of strokes. At the conclusion of any Harvard–Yale race resulting in a victory for Yale, it was usual for the Harvard pundit who had gone to New London filled with a loyal enthusiasm for his college to turn sadly to his nearest companion with the remark that Yale rowed the right stroke and Harvard the wrong one, and that as long as Harvard persisted in rowing the wrong stroke Yale would continue to win.

This pundit might happen to be an old rowing man of the period before the '85 crew, in which case he would add that in his day his crew rowed the way Yale now did, and that Harvard made a great mistake in changing from the old stroke as rowed in his time. He little knew how much thought the Harvard management year after year had given to Yale's manner of rowing, and how hard it tried to instruct the Harvard crews on those very points in the Yale stroke which had resulted in so many of these fast and smooth-rowing Yale crews. If the pundit were an old Harvard oarsman, he was perfectly correct in likening his own crew that he had rowed on to this latest winning Yale crew, provided his crew did happen to be one that rowed well. The only difference perhaps was that the Harvard crew of earlier days rowed their oars more gradually into the water and in so doing had to make a more vigorous catch, while the Yale crews covered their blades with a quick lift of the hands, and took hold of the water firmly but with perhaps less violence, and, moreover, his earlier crew used a shorter slide and consequently a longer body swing than these later Yale crews. If the old Harvard crew rowed well or in other words did what it tried to do with precision and skill, it doubtless was as fast as the winning Yale crew of later days, after allowing for improvements in rigging. Whether the long slide is preferable to the short slide and the deep catch to the shallow one, may always be a debatable question, but when that first-mentioned pundit ascribes the form of this or that Harvard crew of which he disapproved, to any cause except its failure to execute the stroke as it wanted and intended to do, he was generally led into error by a natural feeling of disappointment. In the recover Yale was consistently better, but in spite of constant assertions to the contrary that used to appear in the newspapers, it is a positive fact that no Harvard crew, at least since 1876, has deliberately rushed the recover in order to get in more strokes to the minute, as did the Yale '82 and '83 crews. Whenever they did rush they probably knew it, and certainly they knew that it was wrong.

Looking back at the history of these Harvard crews, it seems clear now that the chief cause of trouble, out of several causes, was in the selection of the stroke oars. Nearly every year the coaches had been unsuccessful in their efforts to find and develop an ideal stroke oar. This was, and still is, the most serious and vital problem that confronts a crew. If the man of the right temperament and physical characteristics for stroke can only be found, and be properly instructed, it is not too much to say that the crew is more than half made. Without the right kind of a stroke oar, it is only through unusual, not to say remarkable support either by No. 7 or No. 6, that any but an ordinary crew can be developed.

The case of the '95 crew was peculiar in that Mr. Watson, having entire charge of the crew and its work, literally made no effort to teach them to row. He was an excellent judge of men's physical capacities, of their vigor and strength, and his method was to change them around until he had put the best men in the boat that were to be had, and then he let them row, and he gave them daily long and carefully planned trips up and down the river, often the full distance without stopping, but he never gave them practical instruction. The result was that each man rowed as he happened to have been taught by former coaches, and they became shaken together into a moderate degree of uniformity in their catch and finish through these long stretches on the river. Compared with the carefully trained Yale crew, the contrast was great, for not in one single particular was their execution of the stroke as good as Yale's.

A little more than a week before the race Mr. Watson sent for George S. Mumford '87, who had coached the Junior class crew which won the class races. Upon his arrival at the quarters Mr. Watson requested him to take the crew and correct its faults. There was no difference of opinion but merely a question of somebody's giving instruction.

The race was rowed down stream on June 28th at a quarter to five in the afternoon. The conditions were fairly good, both crews were at their best, both seemed to be in excellent physical condition. Yale went to the front at once, and at the half mile led by nearly two boat lengths and at the mile had doubled this distance. Harvard rowed the faster and naturally the shorter stroke, but stuck to it with considerable spirit, and in spite of the hopelessness of ever catching Yale except through an accident to the latter crew, rowed on apparently with entire cheerfulness and courage, never showing the slightest indication of going to pieces. Yale's time at the finish was 21 minutes and 30 seconds and Harvard's 22 minutes and 5 seconds, a difference equivalent to about eleven boat lengths.

This has always been reckoned as one of Yale's fastest and best crews, and the following year it was taken to England by Mr. Cook to compete in the Henley Regatta.

An unusual feature this year was the presence of Jennings '98 in both boats in the University and the Freshman races. His rowing was crude, but he was a man of remarkable physique.

The '98 Freshman race was rowed the day before the University race, between crews representing Harvard, Yale and Columbia.

Yale won with great ease, defeating Harvard, who came in second, by eight boat lengths. Columbia was a poor third.

Harvard 1895 Crew

E. N. Wrightington, '97 (164)		F. N. Watriss, L. S.	(174)
Bow		E. H. Fennessy, '96	(169)
J. H. Stillman, '96	(162)	J. R. Bullard, Jr., '96	(160)
J. E. Chatman, '97	(167)	Stroke	
L. D. Shepard, '96	(172)	P. D. Rust, '98	(105)
A. T. Jennings, '98	(184)	Coxswain	

Average weight 170 lbs.

Yale 1895 Crew

R. Armstrong, '95	(155)	J. M. Longacre, '96	(175)
Bow		R. B. Treadway, '96	(173)
H. C. Holcomb, '95	(173)	G. Langford, '97	(163)
W. M. Beard, '96	(177)	Stroke	
W. R. Cross, '96	(195)	T. L. Clarke, '97	(107)
A. W. Dater, '95	(182)	Coxswain	

Average weight 174 lbs.

1896

Cornell won by three boat lengths

Harvard did not row Yale

John Richards Bullard, of Dedham, Massachusetts, class of '96, was reëlected captain after the Harvard–Yale race of '95 at New London.

Watriss was the only regular member of the '95 University crew who did not return the following autumn.

The Harvard–Yale football game played in the autumn of 1894 brought forth much public criticism of the manner of play. Feeling ran high. A prominent old Harvard player was reported as stating that he saw no use in having football games between Harvard and Yale as long as the chief efforts of the teams were devoted to the disabling of the rival players. The Harvard Athletic Committee took the matter up and issued an edict that all future Harvard–Yale contests were hereby abandoned.

It was generally recognized that organized athletics, to be successful, must have the support and interest of the college behind it, and that this interest had lived in the past on the Harvard–Yale contests in rowing, football, and baseball. It was thought that without these contests Harvard would no longer have the incentive to develop even second-rate teams and crews. For after all, it was the prospect of beating Yale that really stirred the blood of the old graduate and the undergraduate alike. Accordingly the Athletic Committee decided to create a new and somewhat artificial athletic interest to take the place of that heretofore felt in the Harvard–Yale contests, and made an alliance with Cornell for a term of two years. This seemed at the time much as though Oxford were to decide to discontinue the annual Oxford–Cambridge boat race and should announce that hereafter the annual event of the rowing season should be an Oxford–University of Edinburgh race.

As a matter of fact the plan of selecting a new chief rival did work well enough in the case of Harvard for one year, but after that the effort required to kill the old traditional rivalry proved to be too great, and the Harvard–Yale contests were resumed almost as a matter of course.

Thus it happened that for the season of 1895–96, the entire Senior year of the class of '96, Yale was left off of the Harvard map.

Harvard was to have its only race with Cornell, but the latter had an agreement with Columbia and the University of Pennsylvania for their usual four-mile contest. Cornell was unwilling to make two separate races of it, and accordingly Harvard was invited to be a fourth in a contest between these crews, and Poughkeepsie on the Hudson River was finally agreed on as the place for the race.

In 1895 Cornell, which had consistently defeated Columbia and University of Pennsylvania in their annual four-mile races, had decided to send its first or best crew to the Henley Regatta.

Cornell drew the Leander eight in the first heat for the Grand Challenge Cup, but the latter failed to start at the word claiming afterwards that it was not ready, and Cornell rowed over the course alone. In its next heat it was defeated by Trinity Hall of

Cambridge. Charles E. Courtney had been Cornell's coach for several years. He had been first an amateur and later a professional sculler at Union Springs, New York State, and as the English experts described it, he taught this Cornell crew to use practically no body swing and to row an exceedingly fast stroke. "The Englishmen relied on the great uniformity and their stronger and more consistent body work, as against the piston action of the Americans. At the White House the race was settled, for Trinity Hall was ahead and the Americans were manifestly tiring. A few strokes further on Cornell fell to pieces, and to all intents and purposes collapsed, leaving Trinity Hall to finish at their ease."

Thus the rowing season of '96 began with Mr. R. C. Watson in charge for the second year of his three-year contract, and a race against three other college crews in prospect. What if Harvard should be fated to bring up the rear of the procession in such a race? The Athletic Committee, having created this Harvard–Cornell alliance, was especially anxious to have the College do well in this, the first year of the two-year Cornell agreement.

The crew went through the usual winter work on rowing machines in the basement of the Cary building on Holmes Field, in the same room where the tank had been constructed. Mr. Watson's regular habit was to go out daily to start the work on the machines and again to give the necessary orders to the crew to stop, and that was all or practically all. He was a man of charming social qualities, greatly beloved by his friends. His interest in athletics was intense. By the members of the older crews of the late '70's and early '80's he was always affectionately referred to as "the Old Man," and as a well-informed adviser and friend, his counsel was welcomed by the captains and by the individual men in the crews of those days.

And now about the first of March public announcement was made that Mr. Watson, with the entire approval of the Athletic Committee, was to start immediately for England for a visit, and that George S. Mumford '87 would coach the crew in his absence. His stay there in fact lasted nearly two months.

Mumford had done considerable coaching while in college, including his own class crew, which won the class races both years he coached it; also, the '88 Freshman crew, which defeated the Columbia Freshmen, and he had been successful with the '96 class crew the season just previous to the present one. He had also coached the '95 University crew for the last week or ten days of its season. After graduating from college he had lived in New York and had only recently come to live in Boston.

He was told that he would have an entirely free hand with the crew, and would be expected to carry it on right up to the race.

After the crew got on the water about the middle of March, Mumford asked George Faulkner, the professional coach, to help him, and this Faulkner consented to do. Faulkner, unfortunately, started in with too much energy and zeal and was soon taken sick, which ended this attempt to get help and advice from the outside.

This time marked the lowest point that Harvard rowing reached. To be sure, Donovan, the "professional" at the Weld boat house, had been able to instill some correct ideas into the minds of a few of the undergraduates who rowed from there on the club crews, but otherwise there was hardly a man on any of the organized crews who rowed well enough to give promise for future University crew material.

Mumford's task was to pick out eight men of the best physique obtainable and teach them to row, beginning with the most elementary instruction.

About the first of May, Mr. Watson returned from England. At first he decided to take over the direction of the crew and so notified Mr. Mumford, but almost immediately reconsidered this action and the Athletic Committee gave out the following statement to the newspapers: "Before going to England at the invitation of Mr. Lehmann, the Oxford coach, to be present at the Oxford–Cambridge regatta, Mr. Watson informed the Athletic Committee that he had asked Mr. Mumford to coach the crew during his absence, and the Committee approved his choice. On his return, finding that satisfactory progress had been made, Mr. Watson wrote a note to Captain Bullard stating that he thought it desirable that no change be made and that Mr. Mumford coach the crew."

About June 8th the crew left for Poughkeepsie, taking the Freshman '99 crew with them.

The situation was a decidedly novel one. Poughkeepsie seemed to be very far away from Cambridge. In fact it took all day to get there from Boston. The climate was unlike that of Cambridge and some of the men on the Harvard crews failed to get acclimated.

Doctor James P. Hutchinson '90 spent a week or more at the quarters and was a great help to the management.

The Cornell crew was clearly Harvard's most dangerous antagonist, as Columbia was neither good to look at nor fast, while Pennsylvania rowed in rather poor form, although apparently able to get considerable speed out of the boat. Harvard was rather the favorite a week before the race and certainly was then at the top of her speed and condition, for in the last week the crew appeared to fall off in both these respects. It was, however, a very lively crew and able to get the boat under way with un-usual quickness and dash.

The crew got quite well together. What this means is difficult to express. It must be experienced to be appreciated. Few crews at Harvard had done it; probably no class crews and not very many University crews. In all organized athletics there is prob-ably no other single act that an athlete enjoys more than rowing in an eight that is well together. All sense of effort is lost and the heavy eight-oared shell travels as if really alive. No boat smaller than an eight will do it.

The race was rowed late in the afternoon down stream on the 26th of June. The start was three miles above the railroad bridge on the west side of the river. Harvard had the position next to the shore, University of Pennsylvania next, Cornell the third position, and Columbia outside.

The start was a fair one, all four crews getting off together. Harvard immediately took the lead, with Cornell and Pennsyl-vania about even and at the half mile Harvard had a length's lead of Cornell, with Pennsylvania half a length behind the latter. Columbia was hopelessly outclassed and lost ground consistently, coming in at the finish thirty lengths behind the winner.

The real race was between Cornell and Harvard. The same lead was maintained by Harvard to the two-mile flag. It was a confort at any rate to feel that the race was on water that gave equal chances to the crews, and not as at New London, where one crew or the other would in the second mile be in eelgrass, and so permit the rival boat to run away from it in the fast current of the channel.

In the next half mile Harvard slowed down and Cornell came up and had a lead of ten or fifteen feet at the two-and-a-half-mile flag. From this point the race was over, for the Harvard crew had lost its power and steadily dropped behind. As they passed under the railroad bridge which marked the three-mile point, Cornell had open water and continued to gain throughout the fourth mile, winning by more than three lengths in 19 minutes and 29 seconds. Harvard had weakened to such an extent that at the end she had fallen back to within a couple of lengths of Pennsylvania, whom earlier in the race she had led by as much as five lengths.

The time made in races on this course cannot be compared with that made at New London, as the body of water is much greater and the current usually swifter than is the Thames River.

Cornell and Harvard rowed practically identical strokes per minute during the race. The Cornell crew appeared to use a slightly shorter slide than Harvard and a good deal more body reach. This Cornell crew, which was the first that Courtney coached after his unsuccessful experience in England at Henley, had an almost perfectly controlled recover showing no evidence of that "professional" recover of the previous Cornell crews.

The Freshman race was rowed two days before the University, between the '99 class crews of Harvard, Cornell, University of Pennsylvania, and Columbia. The referee, armed with a pistol but forgetting its purpose, shouted "Go," which started Cornell off alone, and then he fired his pistol and left the other three crews to try to catch the fortunate leader, in which effort they were unsuccessful. Cornell won by a boat length over Harvard,

with Pennsylvania a good third and Columbia an extremely
poor fourth.

Harvard 1896 Crew

G. S. Derby, '96	(168)	A. A. Sprague, '97	(178)
Bow		J. R. Bullard, '96	(160)
R. M. Townsend, '96	(162)	D. M. Goodrich, '98	(163)
J. H. Perkins, '98	(169)	Stroke	
S. Hollister, '97	(173)	P. D. Rust, '96	(110)
E. H. Fennessy, '96	(170)	Coxswain	

Average weight 168 lbs.

Cornell 1896 Crew

I. C. Ludlum, '98	(160)	E. O. Spillman, '97	(163)
Bow		L. L. Tatum, '97	(160)
W. T. Cresswell, '97	(160)	F. A. Briggs, '98	(130)
C. S. Moore, '98	(163)	Stroke	
F. W. Freeborn, '97	(176)	F. D. Colson, '97	(103)
E. J. Savage, '98	(160)	Coxswain	

Average weight 159 lbs.

1897

Cornell first, Yale second, Harvard third

David Marvin Goodrich, the stroke, had been elected captain. He was of the class of 1898 and from Akron, Ohio.

At a consultation of some old Harvard oarsmen it was agreed between them and the captain and Mr. Mumford that the latter should coach the crew this year. The work for the season was planned out by the captain and coach in a general way, they sent for O'Dea, a professional who later coached Wisconsin University crew, with a view to employing him as an assistant.

At this stage of the proceedings Mr. Watson decided to take up himself the burden of his third and last year under the agreement or contract. His health at this time had begun to fail, but his devotion to the cause and his courage prompted him to attempt a task that was clearly beyond his strength. It is certain that consideration for his friends, who had placed him in the position and bound him by a three-year contract, was a potent argument with him to see it through.

And now one of these friends who had been associated with him on the Graduate Rowing Committee in 1888, Mr. Francis Peabody, Jr., came forward with the suggestion that Mr. Lehmann be invited over from England to take charge of Harvard rowing.

The two men had been friends in their undergraduate days in Cambridge, England, and Mr. Lehmann was now to make his home in Peabody's house in Milton, Massachusetts, for the better part of the next two years.

[112]

of the men was, therefore, decided on with a view to the Yale race.

William S. Bryant '84, the stroke of the successful Senior crew in the class races of this year, rowed stroke in the University crew in its race with Columbia, with Captain Perkins rowing at No. 7. These two men now exchanged seats, — Perkins returning to stroke, where he had rowed the year before, and Bryant taking his seat at No. 7; Borland, No. 2, was moved down to occupy No. 5 seat in the boat, while the men formerly rowing at No. 5 and bow were dropped out, the vacant positions at bow and No. 2 being taken by J. R. Yocom '85 and A. Keith '85, respectively, two comparatively green men who had come to New London with the crew as substitutes.

With all Harvard crews up to 1900, the system of training resulted in developing with more or less success eight men fit to sit in the University boat, and eight men only. The employment of substitutes at the last moment was always dangerous, as they seldom or never had had the same training that the regular men had undergone and were never taken into the crew except under the pressure of absolute necessity. In this case the boat was greatly improved by restoring Perkins to his old seat at stroke, and during the short time remaining for practice before the Yale race, the men did succeed in getting fairly well together. The fact that Harvard was not defeated until the third mile was reached may be considered a direct tribute to the rowing ability of Captain Perkins, the stroke.

In every decade, one or two oarsmen have stood out as preeminent amongst their associates, and Perkins '84 was one of these. In power, rowing form, watermanship, and effectiveness

RUDOLPH C. LEHMANN

From an English cartoon published in 1898

Rudolph Chambers Lehmann occupied at this time so prominent a position as a coach and adviser of eight-oared crews in England that he was at that time better known as a rowing authority in this country than any other Englishman before or since who had confined himself entirely to his home waters. Forty years of age, a good after-dinner speaker and a cultivated gentleman, his popularity was a tribute to his charming social qualities.

It is probable that Mr. Lehmann little understood the nature of the problem before him when he arrived in this country.

Although eight-oared rowing had already been practised here since 1876, we in this country were at least twenty years behind England in this particular sport. That is to say, it was not until long after his time that the preparatory schools here had generally taken it up and our college oarsmen seriously attempted to compete after graduation in regattas with other well-organized and trained eight-oared crews, manned by oarsmen who had already attained distinction on college eights. In England an almost unlimited amount of material made up of fairly well-trained men was at hand both at Oxford and Cambridge, from which to select the eights which were to represent those Universities in their annual race. The records of these men were known and had been proved by racing in eights for years past in the schools and colleges. In fact in coaching English crews, Mr. Lehmann had himself little to do with selecting his eight, as its make-up became more or less a matter of course by a previous process of elimination. He personally coached the crew for but a comparatively short time before the race, and might suggest the removal of one man here or to try another in some seat in the boat. It is probable that if he were to come to Harvard now he would find his task on the whole much as it was at Oxford in 1896. But in 1896 Harvard crews were not selected by any other process of elimination than that of passing over the obviously unfit men from a single crew, the Freshmen of the previous season, and laboring with the selected few over those fundamentals which should have been already familiar to them all.

Although a Cambridge graduate himself, he had gone to Oxford after a long series of annual victories for Cambridge, in the true spirit of real sportsmanship, and as a result Oxford had begun to turn out winning crews.

He had seen an English crew victorious at Henley over Yale in 1896 coached by Mr. Cook, and another English crew defeat Cornell coached by Courtney in 1895, and he gladly accepted the suggestion that now came to him, to show Harvard how to turn out crews that would do what these English crews had done.

When he arrived in the autumn (November 12, 1896), he may have expected to look the ground over, pick the most likely men out of Harvard's rowing material, show them in a general way what to practise at during the winter and spring, and then come back before the race to finish them off. If this was indeed his original plan, he at once found it necessary to modify it considerably. The only possible men he found were those left over from the 1896 University crew and from the '99 Freshman boat.

The task of teaching them to row like the English eights, with the shorter slide and the extremely long body swing, was one that he found he could not delegate to any one else. Accordingly he did all the coaching himself in the early preliminary work of the crew, as well as in its final stages, which was a very different experience from that he previously had had under the conditions in England, and one which he doubtless little realized he was in for when he generously offered his services.

Yale in 1896 having no Harvard race had entered the Henley Regatta, following the example of Cornell the year before. While Harvard was racing Cornell in the Poughkeepsie Regatta, Yale, with substantially the same crew that had defeated Harvard the previous year, found herself competing with Leander in one of the preliminary heats for the Grand Challenge Cup. The English account states that the Yale crew was composed of very powerful material, but did not succeed in getting together, and Leander beat them with ease. All accounts seem to agree that Yale was in poor physical condition at the time of the race.

Athletic relations with Yale for 1897 renewed themselves pretty much as if nothing had ever happened, but we still had another year of our two-year contract with Cornell. Harvard had to row Cornell and wanted to row Yale, and Yale was willing to meet them both in a contest of three crews, but declined to meet Cornell's other competitors. Cornell agreed to row two races on condition that the race with Harvard and Yale be at Poughkeepsie so that she could herself row a second race there with Columbia and University of Pennsylvania without moving her headquarters. Thus a Harvard–Yale–Cornell race was arranged.

Except for a short visit to England in the middle of the winter Mr. Lehmann worked over the crew continuously until the race.

He sought for little actual help from Harvard's old coaches, but Messrs. James J. Storrow and Mumford were with him frequently on the launch, and the latter at his invitation spent the week before the race as a visitor at Poughkeepsie.

The newspapers all through the year gave an unusual amount of their space to news about the English coach and the Harvard crew, and on the whole their attitude was friendly and showed less disposition to criticize Harvard for what was called her "un-American" proceeding than might have been expected.

The Harvard crew never really appeared to be very fast either before or after it reached its quarters on the Hudson River, but everybody, the crew, the College, and the graduates, had the most complete confidence in Mr. Lehmann and in the outcome of the race.

Mr. Lehmann expressed himself as satisfied at times with the form of the crew, and with the degree of success it attained in mastering the long English body swing, but there is no doubt that the men lay back at the finish excessively far, so much so as to exaggerate this characteristic of English crews. The boat used was an English shell with the men seated not directly over the keel, but port men on starboard side of the center and starboard men on port side, balancing each other. Thole pins were used as on the Oxford shells, and not oarlocks.

Yale did her training just previous to the race at her old quarters at New London and her crew was brought to Poughkeepsie by Mr. Cook two days before the race. Cook personally coached the crew this year throughout the entire season.

Cornell appeared to row with longer slides than the year before and on the whole looked smoother, better together, and faster.

The race was rowed down stream on June 25th in the afternoon. Yale had the position nearest the west shore of the river, Cornell the center, and Harvard the outside course.

When the crews started it was obvious almost at once that

HARVARD, '97, CREW AT POUGHKEEPSIE

Showing men seated on opposite sides of keel

Cornell had the fastest crew, and also that the race was between her and Yale. Cornell led Yale by nearly a length at the first half-mile flag and Harvard was nearly another length behind. Cornell continued to gain slowly but steadily, leading Yale at the finish by four boat lengths. The Harvard crew in the last half mile fell behind very rapidly and finally struggled over the finish line in bad shape seven or eight lengths behind Yale.

Cornell a few days later easily defeated Columbia and the University of Pennsylvania.

The condition of the Harvard crew again showed that the men had been unable to contend with the climate of Poughkeepsie. Looking after their condition and their food had proved a heavy and doubtless an unaccustomed task for Mr. Lehmann. The daily duty of ordering their meals was one he little enjoyed, and he more than once informed the steward at the quarters that he preferred coaching the crews to marketing for them.

At the Harvard Commencement this year, as an expression of appreciation of our obligation to Mr. Lehmann, and of the high regard in which he was held as an educated gentleman and sportsman, Harvard University conferred upon him the Honorary Degree of Master of Arts, and President Eliot in bestowing it stated that he was glad to pay this tribute to an English University man and a scholar "who brought to us from a sister university the best traditions of manly English sport."

The Freshman 1900 race was rowed on June 23d, two days before the University race, between the crews of Harvard, Yale, and Cornell.

Yale won, leading Harvard by a couple of lengths at the finish, with Harvard second and Cornell third by a length.

Mr. Edward C. Storrow '89 coached the Harvard Freshman crew, and under Mr. Lehmann's directions made every effort to carry out the latter's ideas. To this extent was an attempt being made to carry on and continue Mr. Lehmann's work after he should have returned again to England.

Harvard 1897 Crew

G. D. Marvin, '99	(160)	John F. Perkins, '99	(174)
Bow		D. M. Goodrich, '98	(165)
C. C. Bull, '98	(165)	E. A. Boardman, Jr., '99	(155)
E. N. Wrightington, '97	(165)	Stroke	
A. A. Sprague, '97	(178)	R. S. Huidekoper, '98	(100)
James H. Perkins, '98	(170)	Coxswain	

Average weight 167 lbs.

Cornell 1897 Crew

S. W. Wakeman, '99	(165)	E. O. Spillman, '97	(166)
Bow		E. J. Savage, '98	(162)
W. Bentley, '98	(160)	F. A. Briggs, '98	(134)
C. S. Moore, '98	(168)	Stroke	
A. C. King, '99	(168)	F. D. Colson, '97	(105)
M. M. Odell, '97	(162)	Coxswain	

Average weight 160½ lbs.

Yale 1897 Crew

D. F. ROGERS, '98	(165)	F. W. ALLEN, 'oo	(180)
Bow		W. E. S. GRISWOLD, '99	(175)
P. WHITNEY, '98	(164)	G. LANGFORD, '97	(164)
H. G. CAMPBELL, '97	(175)	Stroke	
J. C. GREENWAY, 'oo	(174)	L. GREEN, '99	(100)
P. H. BAILEY, '97	(180)	Coxswain	

Average weight 172 lbs.

1898

Cornell first, Yale second, Harvard third

David M. Goodrich, class of '98, was reëlected captain of the crew.

Mr. Lehmann's original hope and intention doubtless was to put Harvard's rowing on a good foundation, enable her to win her race in 1897, and thereafter perhaps make an occasional visit from year to year to help keep things going. After the defeat at Poughkeepsie he was convinced that he had made an unfortunate selection of his men, that some of them had been deficient in stamina and in their nervous organization, and he was quite keen to make another attempt. His offer to coach the next year was gratefully accepted.

An event had taken place the previous year of immense importance in Harvard's athletic history, in the appointment by the President of Professor Hollis as Chairman of the Athletic Committee. Professor Ira N. Hollis, of the Department of Engineering at the University, was a graduate of and later had been an instructor in the Naval Academy at Annapolis. He completely changed the position of the Athletic Committee, gave it an independent standing, put it in a place of real authority, and made it act in whole-hearted sympathy with undergraduate athletic activities. He personally succeeded in interesting various important members of the Faculty, including the President, in the intercollegiate contests themselves and, an heretofore unheard-of achievement, conducted the President, Mr. Eliot, to witness football games and perhaps to enjoy them.

Professor Hollis at the same time was superintending the development of the immense salt marsh on the south side of the Charles River now known as "Soldiers' Field" and a few years later planned and carried out the construction of the Stadium.

All of the changes wrought by him in the relations between students and Faculty came about so imperceptibly that few Harvard men, even those who would naturally be well informed, realized at the time how great they were and how valuable was his work.

Mr. Lehmann believed that in order to develop material for the University crew, a great many more men should be encouraged to row for the sport of the thing, and that instead of training eight men through the season to row in the University crew, if one hundred or two hundred men could only be taught to row, and to practise in eight-oared shells through the spring season — and perhaps train for local races — a greater interest would be created in rowing as a sport, and consequently more material would be available for the University crew. This would be more like the system prevailing in England, under which University crews there were selected. He decided to use the class races this year as a try-out for the University crew candidates, and in order to increase the number of crews and to create more racing and general interest, the Weld boat club organized four class crews from among its members and an eight from the Law School as well, and arranged for this Weld class race of five crews in all, to take place the day before the regular class races. The fact that the race was rowed in a storm and that all five crews sank, served to mar considerably the effect of this first race however.

The class crews were developed under excellent conditions and intense rivalry. Mr. Edward C. Storrow '89 coached the Fresh-

[121]

6

men, James J. Storrow, George S. Mumford, and T. Nelson Perkins the other three. They proved to be unusually good crews, and the race on April 16th was well rowed and won by the Sophomores of the class of 1900, coached by James J. Storrow.

Captain Goodrich was extremely anxious to have Mr. Lehmann associate some Harvard man with him in coaching the University crew and picking the men, especially with a view to continuing the work of this year for the future without any break. Nothing came of this, however, and on April 21st the Spanish War breaking out, Captain Goodrich, having already resigned, left College to join the Rough Riders.

James H. Perkins, of Milton, Massachusetts, class of '98, was elected captain of the University crew immediately after the class races. Perkins was a brother of Thomas Nelson Perkins, captain of the successful '91 crew.

The Spanish War affected Harvard College and college crews, as it influenced all other activities in the United States during this spring and early summer. Several promising candidates followed Goodrich's example and enlisted in the Army or Navy.

Mr. Lehmann selected two eights after the class races to constitute the Varsity squad, from the most promising men to be found in the class crews.

The Harvard–Yale race having been reëstablished the year before, arrangements were made to row it as usual over the four-mile course at New London, and because of Cornell's victory over both the other colleges the previous season, Cornell was asked to join them for this year and make the contest again a three-cornered one. This suggestion was accepted, although it involved for Cornell one four-mile race at New London and another, this time at Saratoga, very few days later.

The progress of the Harvard crew during the spring season was discouraging to as great a degree as the previous season had appeared to be the reverse. Mr. Lehmann frequently stated that he proposed this year to have a crew that would row four miles without giving out; that no matter how fast the other crews were, and no matter how far they might get ahead at first, he proposed that Harvard should still have some power and life left, to race them over the last mile of the course. As a matter of fact the crew proved to be a slow one, and even before it left for New London was regarded by the College without enthusiasm or confidence.

The race was to be rowed a little earlier in the season than usual, out of consideration for Cornell's engagement with Columbia, University of Pennsylvania, and University of Wisconsin. It was set for June 22d and the three crews were to row in lanes marked out by buoys, starting close to the west bank and curving the course around the fatal eelgrass flats in the second mile.

A violent storm completely scattered the buoys before the hour set for the race and after waiting all day for a fair course and smooth water, the crews were ordered to be ready to start on the day following.

The race was rowed shortly after noon down stream on June 23d. Cornell had the inside position close to the bank, Yale the middle, and Harvard the most easterly course. The buoys, which had been anchored to mark the lanes and were scattered about the river by the storm, had all by this time either been successfully replaced or removed altogether from the course.

[123]

The race was close between Yale and Cornell for the first half mile, Yale having a slight lead at first, but the two boats were practically even most of this distance, with Harvard falling steadily to the rear. From this point Cornell gradually drew ahead of Yale and led her by six seconds at the mile, where Harvard was fifteen seconds behind the leader. At the third mile Cornell led Yale by fifteen seconds and Harvard by forty-four. The relative positions remained unchanged in the last mile and Cornell won in 23 minutes 48 seconds, defeating Yale by nearly four boat lengths and Harvard by thirteen.

Harvard was not a good racing crew, although possibly composed of better material than the year before. Stroke had a noticeable hang at the full reach, and if just the right man had been found for this position, the crew might have been pretty good. They finished in excellent condition, as was expected of them.

Cornell was defeated by the University of Pennsylvania in the race at Saratoga a few days later, and the obviously poor condition of some of her men in that race was one of the results of her good sporting spirit in giving Harvard and Yale this one more chance to beat her great crew, for it was much the same crew that had rowed in 1896 and 1897. Cornell's experience in this effort to row two hard four-mile races within a few days of each other recalled Harvard's experience in a similar attempt in 1886 and again in 1887.

Mr. Lehmann's work for Harvard was over, but he left a lasting impression upon eight-oared rowing, not at Harvard alone but all over the country. He left Harvard on a new and vastly improved rowing basis. It is impossible to imagine a greater contrast than

CORNELL CREWS IN 1899 AT PRACTICE

An excellent illustration of the proper way to apply the power with the shoulders

that between the low ebb to which rowing there had sunk at the beginning of 1896 and the keen general interest displayed in the sport two or three years later.

During his stay at Harvard, all groups of graduates with divergent views as to the conduct and the rowing of the University crew were united never again to come to serious disagreement.

Eight-oared rowing in other colleges and preparatory schools became much more general at this time and the popular interest that he created in the sport was one of the chief causes that contributed to this.

His two crews were defeated by faster ones, and of course this was a bitter disappointment, but it is only fair to say that he had underrated both Cook and Courtney because of their respective failures in England in 1896 and 1895, which took place under his own eyes. They were both able, intelligent men, and learned a whole lot in England, besides being familiar with the best rowing that America afforded. They also had had to contend against a different climate and unaccustomed conditions while in England, as he in 1897 had himself to struggle with on the banks of the Hudson River.

The Freshman race was rowed at New London on the same day as the University race, between the class of 1901 crews of Harvard, Yale, and Cornell. Yale and Harvard were very nearly tied for first place, Yale winning by perhaps ten feet. Cornell was a boat length behind in third place. Edward C. Storrow coached the Harvard Freshmen.

Harvard 1898 Crew

G. S. Derby, M. S.	(161)	James H. Perkins, '98	(172)
Bow		N. Biddle, '00	(160)
J. D. Kernan, '00	(169)	F. Dobyns, '98	(151)
E. Wadsworth, '98	(164)	Stroke	
F. L. Higginson, Jr., '00	(164)	G. R. Orton, Gr. Stu.	(103)
C. L. Harding, '00	(163)	Coxswain	

Average weight 163 lbs.

Cornell 1898 Crew

W. C. Dalzell, '99	(160)	R. W. Beardslee, '00	(150)
Bow		E. J. Savage, '98	(170)
W. Bentley, '98	(160)	F. A. Briggs, '98	(138)
S. W. Wakeman, '99	(168)	Stroke	
T. D. Bailey, '99	(169)	F. D. Colson, Gr. Stu.	(112)
C. S. Moore, '98	(169)	Coxswain	

Average weight 160½ lbs.

Yale 1898 Crew

Payne Whitney, '98	(164)	F. W. Allen, '00	(181)
Bow		J. C. Greenleaf, '99	(170)
H. P. Wickes, '00	(168)	W. B. Williams, '00	(157)
J. P. Brock, '00	(183)	Stroke	
R. P. Flint, '99	(167)	J. McL. Walton, '99	(113)
J. D. Niedeken, '00	(170)	Coxswain	

Average weight 170 lbs.

Colson, the coxswain and captain of the Cornell crew this year, is the same who coached the Harvard crew five or six years later.

1899

Harvard won by six boat lengths

Francis Lee Higginson, Jr., was elected captain of the crew. Higginson was a 1900 man and lived in Boston. He prepared for college at Groton School.

A new world now opened to Harvard rowing men, both in respect to its physical conditions and to the spirit that animated the graduates in supporting unanimously the crew management.

All along the banks of the Charles River a change was taking place, in converting the ill-looking marshes that fringed the river bank, by the construction of driveways and the planting of trees, into what might almost be considered a parkway through which the river wound. It was some years later that the dam was constructed which ended the course on the river as a tideway, but even at this time the changes were so great as to add considerably to the pleasure of rowing on the Charles. The new University boat house, donated by the Harvard Club of New York City, was under construction on the south bank just above the Boylston Street bridge on the edge of the new Soldiers Field. The name Newell boat house is also sometimes given it in memory of Marshall Newell '93, who rowed in several Harvard crews and met a tragic death shortly before this time. This boat house, by the way, was destroyed by fire through carelessness on the part of some of the workmen before it was entirely completed, and involved also in its destruction a new launch given in memory of Mr. Frank Thomson of Philadelphia by his children, which had been hauled up on the bank close to the building. Another building was immediately begun and covered entirely with slate on the outside to afford greater protection from fire, and another launch was speedily provided and rechristened the "John Harvard."

The coming of Mr. Lehmann two years before served to unite all groups of graduates with divergent views, and after his time the captains and the coaches have been loyally supported by the entire body of graduates. The many differences of opinion that may have arisen have been of minor importance and helped, by creating friendly discussion, to increase the interest among the graduates at large and to aid the development of the crews.

Some New York graduates this year inspired by desire to help all they could to give Harvard a winning crew, had made up a considerable sum of money for the purpose of building a special boat of unusual design and construction, which it was hoped would be faster than any eight-oared shell then known. The attempt proved to be a failure, as the boat as constructed could not possibly be rowed by any crew no matter how skillful it might be, but the spirit in which the contribution was made was highly gratifying to the crew.

Not only were many more crews to be seen on the river at this time than ever before, but the school boy rowing in the Boston schools began to take on considerable importance, and the training some of these boys obtained helped Harvard crews very much in future years.

Edward Cabot Storrow '89 was selected to coach the crew. He had helped Mr. Lehmann for the two years previous, relieving the latter entirely from the duties of looking after the Freshman

EDWARD C. STORROW, '89

On the Coaching Launch "John Harvard" at New London, 1899

crews, and had now become an excellent instructor. During his undergraduate days he had been one of the best oarsmen in College, had been captain of the '88 crew, had rowed stroke on the '87 crew, and in the race against Columbia that year, Harvard established the record of 20 minutes and 15 seconds, which was only five seconds slower than the record made by the famous Yale crew of '88, which stood unbeaten for nearly thirty years.

Storrow was a most careful and painstaking coach. He fully appreciated the advantages that previous Yale crews had in their superiority over Harvard crews in the matter of recover. He succeeded this year in developing a crew that had good driving power, kept well together and showed excellent control of the recover, so as to be able to row the four miles without checking the boat on each stroke, as Harvard crews had been so constantly doing year after year.

Thanks partly to Mr. Lehmann's efforts there was abundant material for possible University men, both at the Weld boat house and at the University boat house, and there was no difficulty in preparing excellent crews to compete in preliminary races, with a view to selecting the University candidates.

The spring season began with the regular class crews, Senior, Junior, and Sophomore, besides a number of Freshman crews. The Weld and Newell boat clubs also had their respective class crews, and a Law School crew likewise rowed from the Weld. The 1900 class crew, then Juniors, with Higginson No. 7, Biddle No. 5, and Harding No. 2, proved to be the fastest and won the regular race for the Beacon cup on April 14th. After the class races, the candidates for the University crew squad were selected and put into two trial eights arranged to be as even as possible. These crews had their race about two weeks later. About the first of May, the University crew squad was definitely selected and work was begun on the drilling of the crew, with about eight weeks' time for preparation before the race with Yale on June 29th.

Of the former Harvard coaches, Messrs. James J. Storrow '85 and George S. Mumford '87, who had both coöperated closely with Mr. Lehmann, were in frequent consultation with the captain and the coach throughout the year.

Cornell had definitely abandoned its effort to row two four-mile races within a week of each other, and the Harvard–Yale contests were now resumed under conditions similar to those of other years, but with one difference. Mr. Lehmann had come to this country without any prejudices and certainly had no reason to look upon Yale with unfriendly eyes. In consequence the relations which he established between the Harvard camp and the Yale camp were quite different from those of other years. Mr. Robert J. Cook also severed his connection with Yale rowing after the 1898 race. During the twenty-seven years between 1872 and 1898, except for the '82 and '83 crews, his control of Yale's rowing had been nearly absolute. This year Yale was coached by Dr. E. F. Gallaudet, who was stroke of the Yale University crews of '92 and '93. Dr. Gallaudet was assisted by John Kennedy, a professional oarsman and boat rigger of considerable reputation.

At New London also the conditions had become quite different from those of earlier years. The New York, New Haven & Hartford Railroad had this year completed its line from New London to Norwich, and on to Worcester, Mass., skirting the East Shore of the Thames River for the entire length of the four-mile course.

Left to right: John Forbes Perkins, Harvard, '99; George St. John Sheffield, of Yale; Robert J. Cook, Yale '76; George S. Mumford, Harvard '87; Robert F. Herrick, Harvard '90. At New London, June 1908. From a photograph by *Boston Globe*.

They, as well as the New London & Northern Railroad people, constructed special cars for use in observation trains for the Harvard–Yale races which were a great improvement over the old flat cars with temporary benches erected on top of them, and also enabled both railroads to run much longer trains than under the old system. It was thus possible to accommodate several thousand spectators on the trains, and there was no longer any excuse for running a fleet of steam boats loaded with spectators to charge upon and sometimes surround the competing crews from start to finish of their long four miles.

The United States Congress passed an act enabling Government officials to create a clear course for racing boats and to compel spectators to anchor their craft so as not to interfere with races, or to unduly disturb the water and annoy the crews. From this time on only the official boats and the coaching launches followed the crews during their races, and such scenes of confusion as had been witnessed in the early '90's were no longer possible.

When the crews went to New London, they carried with them four-oared shells for the use of the substitutes, as arrangements had been made for a race of second crews between Harvard and Yale, made up of the four substitutes for the University crews. In later years these second fours grew to be second eights, and they in turn required their substitutes so that the old method of having a couple of untrained substitutes for the University crews was from this time definitely abandoned. Messrs. James J. Storrow and Mumford were at the quarters during nearly the whole of the stay at New London. The former gave his personal attention to the Freshman crew of 1902, while Mumford assisted Edward C. Storrow more or less with the University crew.

The University race was rowed down stream on June 29th in the afternoon. Mr. William A. Meikleham, Columbia '86, acted as referee, and has continued ever since to referee Harvard–Yale races. Meikleham before this had been referee in the '91 race, and also in 1897 and 1898. He was captain of the famous Columbia crew which defeated Harvard in his Senior year, certainly the best of Columbia's crews of former days.

The conditions were good. The water was smooth and the tide fairly high, but not excessively strong. Harvard had the west course and Yale the east or Groton side of the river. The start was perfectly even, both crews rowing about thirty-seven strokes to the minute. The official records show that Yale led Harvard by one second at the half-mile flag, but in watching the crews it seemed as though Harvard was holding her own without any great difficulty, and that it was Yale that was making the more violent effort to keep up. Throughout the race the two crews rowed almost identical strokes to the minute. They both showed good control of the recover, and the race proved to be a fair test of skill and power, with little to choose between the two crews as to form. In approaching the mile flag Harvard began to draw ahead, apparently at that point leading Yale by one second, and this lead was increased until the second mile when Yale was seven seconds behind Harvard. During the next mile there was little relative change in the position of the two crews, but after the third-mile flag was passed Harvard steadily increased her lead until the finish, which she reached 21 seconds ahead of Yale. Her time for the four miles was 20 minutes $52\frac{1}{2}$ seconds.

This was the first victory that a Harvard University crew had won since 1891. Both Harvard and Yale had excellent crews.

The race was a real race and both crews were in good condition and finished without the signs of physical collapse which had been so apparent in some other years.

Dr. Eugene A. Darling, class of '90, remained with the Harvard crew all the time it was at New London, and might almost be called its physical director. In former years doctors had visited the quarters and Dr. William Conant '79, especially, had given up several days for three or four successive years to looking out for Harvard crews, but this was the first year in which a doctor had been present to watch the condition of the men during their entire stay at New London. He carried on an interesting investigation with regard to the growth and action of hearts and the action of kidneys under special strains, and as to the effect of diets on the rowing men, particularly with a view to determining the amount and quality of food best suited to keeping them in condition. The results of his investigations proved to be of very great interest and considerable importance. It seems certain now that if only a Dr. Darling had been on hand with some of the Harvard crews of other years, while the results of many of those races might not have been different, some of them at any rate would have been much closer contests, particularly during their fourth miles.

The four-oared race for substitutes, which was called the race of the Second University crews, took place about four o'clock the same afternoon as the University race. The distance was for two miles and rowed down stream, finishing at the Navy Yard. This race, which, with the Freshman race immediately after it, was rowed under very fast conditions, proved to be an easy victory for the Harvard crew, which led from the start, finishing fifteen seconds ahead of Yale. The time, 10 minutes 51 seconds, remained a record for several years.

The Freshman race was rowed over the second two miles of the course. At the end of the first mile Yale led by nearly a boat length. In the second mile, which corresponded to the last mile in the four-mile course, both crews were seriously interfered with by a large steam boat. Whether Yale suffered more than Harvard is uncertain, but at any rate she fell behind her Crimson rival and was beaten by about two boat lengths. Harvard's time was 9 minutes 33½ seconds, which established a new record for two-mile Freshman races at New London. Thus Harvard had defeated Yale in three races in one day, certainly an unheard-of achievement, and a great tribute to Captain Higginson's management of affairs.

Harvard *1899* Crew

C. L. Harding, '00 (161) Bow

D. B. Evans, '01 (159)

C. B. Wood, '98, L. S. (173)

N. W. Tilton, '00 (175)

J. Lawrence, Jr., '01 (172)

H. Bancroft, '98, L. S. (173)

C. W. Sheafe, '98, L. S. (168)

F. L. Higginson, Jr., '00 (161) Stroke

H. A. Wadleigh, '00 (101) Coxswain

Average weight 167½ lbs.

Twenty Harvard Crews

Yale 1899 Crew

J. C. GREENLEAF, '99 (170)   F. W. ALLEN, '00 (181)
Bow   J. H. NIEDEKEN, '00 (170)
H. P. WICKES, '00 (168)   W. B. WILLIAMS, '00 (157)
W. E. S. GRISWOLD, '00 (175)   Stroke
R. P. FLINT, '99 (167)   J. McL. WALTON, '99 (113)
F. G. BROWN, JR., '00 (190)   Coxswain

Average weight 172 lbs.

Harvard 1899 Four-Oared Crew

L. ENDICOTT, '01 (158)   R. F. BLAKE, '99 (160)
Bow   Stroke
JOHN F. PERKINS, '99 (177)   R. H. HOWE, JR., '01 (105)
J. D. KERNAN, '00 (170)   Coxswain

1900

Yale won

Francis Lee Higginson, Jr., 1900, was reëlected captain of the University crew. Peter Higginson, as he was known to his friends, had rowed stroke the year before. The work of the crew was a repetition of that of the year before, with the same coach, Mr. Edward C. Storrow.

The new boat house was now finally completed and occupied.

The theory of competing crews from which to select candidates for the University crew was carried a step farther, and the management decided to bring it to its logical conclusion by making the final selection of class crews from the winners in contests between the respective class crews of the Weld and Newell boat clubs. Thus, the old custom of having a real representative class crew from each class, irrespective of clubs, was abandoned. Each club had its class crews, thus making at least two crews in each class to be tried for by candidates. The club crews in each class first rowed a series of dual races to determine which club should represent each class in the regular class races for the Beacon cup. Class rivalry had done much in the past to stimulate interest in the crews, and when Harvard rowing was at its lowest, the class crews furnished about the only rowing contests which were able to awaken any signs of enthusiasm or excitement amongst the undergraduates. This new move caused at the time considerable criticism among the undergraduates, and was later felt to have been a mistake, in that it largely killed class competition and interest by substituting for a natural class rivalry the artificial rivalry of the two boat clubs. The final races for the Beacon cup this year, which were rowed on April 13th, were again won by 1900, then Seniors, with Harding at stroke and Higginson at No. 7, making the third time this class had won, a record unequalled before or since by any other class.

After these class races, the same program was followed as the year before. Trial eights were formed which rowed for about two weeks, and then the University squad was definitely graded into a first and second crew. From the time of grading, it made very rapid progress, with the exception of a slump of a few days when the crew was trying out a new boat designed by Clinton R. Crane.

In the early part of this year efforts had been made to see if some improvement in model or design could not be made to increase the speed of the shell. With this in view, consultations were held with Mr. Crane, the well-known New York yacht designer. Full-sized drawings of various good shells were submitted, and he worked on them during the early winter months. Some of his comments were rather interesting. Among other things, he expressed surprise that the rule-of-thumb methods of our boat builders had approached so closely to scientific perfection. He also expressed surprise that eight men with their oars in the water about one-third of the time should be able to develop sufficient power to force a boat along at the pace that they did. The boat he designed was fast, but unusually difficult to row steadily, and the crew had great trouble in learning to hold it up.

At the time the crew went to New London it was made up of the following men: stroke, F. L. Higginson, 1900; No. 7, Charles M. Sheafe of '98, then in the Law School; No. 6, Hugh Bancroft of '98, then in the Law School; No. 5, W. E. Ladd, 1902; No. 4, W. Shuebruck, 1902; No. 3, Clement B. Wood of '98, then in the Law School; No. 2, Charles L. Harding, 1900; bow, Nicholas Biddle, 1900.

The crew developed better form and greater speed than the year before, and was very well together indeed. Higginson as stroke was able by this time to keep his crew well in hand, and he himself had unusual driving power. He was also a smooth, well-finished oarsman and is probably entitled to rank among Harvard's best stroke oars. Three of the men behind him, Sheafe, Bancroft, and Wood, all in the Law School, had had an unusual amount of rowing experience. They had begun their rowing education under Donovan, the "professional," at the Weld boat club nearly six years before. Probably there was no man in the boat who was not an exceptionally finished oarsman, and it is doubtful if Harvard has ever turned out a more perfect rowing crew than was this crew at this time. In later years under the system of choosing the crew from a very large number of candidates, it is quite possible that the material may at times be better than it was at this period, but the careful training over every detail of the stroke that the Yale crews had been accustomed to receive, and that this Harvard crew had also undergone, made it possible for them to execute those details more accurately and with greater precision than the later crews. At any rate, Harvard never turned out a more perfect working machine than was this 1900 crew at the end of the week previous to the race.

The dangerous second mile of the course, the so-called eelgrass mile, was made more fair by arranging a curve for the crews during this mile so that both boats would be wholly in the channel, and

Francis L. Higginson, Jr., Class of 1900
in his Senior Year

HARVARD, 1900, CREW AT NEW LONDON, WITH HIGGINSON AT STROKE

Excellent illustration of dash and life

thereafter it was possible to row under equal conditions, if only the coxswain of the crew having the east course, followed instructions and did not try disastrous short cuts across the mud flats.

Five days before the Yale race Captain Higginson, while standing near the quarters tossing a tennis ball, in some manner broke his leg and this accident proved to be a veritable tragedy. It was believed that Yale was outclassed by Harvard, and the result of a race between this Harvard crew and Yale under equal conditions for both crews was never for a moment in doubt in the minds of the Harvard management, and now the boat had to be rearranged. A new stroke was selected, Charles L. Harding, 1900, who had been rowing at No. 2. Harding's place at No. 2 was taken by Harold Bullard, class of '02.

Harding proved to be an excellent stroke, and the crew made such good use of the few days intervening before the race that it began to look as though Harvard might be successful in spite of the loss of Higginson, although as a rule the loss of a good stroke oar completely alters the style of any crew.

The race was rowed down stream on June 28th about 1.30 in the afternoon. The atmosphere was extremely close and the sun beat down on the heads of the Harvard crew for nearly three-quarters of an hour, as it waited at the start, before the Yale eight put in its appearance. Such a strain on the men was a very severe test of their nervous energy.

When the race finally started it seemed quite clear that the Harvard crew was about as good as ever. The first part was extremely even, they were both good crews and rowed about equally fast. They made a hard fight of it, and by the time they reached the two-and-one-half-mile mark both seemed to be fairly tired.

Shortly after this stage, with Yale in the lead by about a half length, it was remarked by those who were following, that Harding the Harvard stroke was showing signs of distress. It was learned afterwards that from this point on he was actually unconscious of what was happening, but continued sliding back and forth automatically at the rather slow rate of twenty-nine strokes to the minute. In spite of this, the other seven men were able to put on enough extra power to come up with and pass Yale at this point, so that they led by about a length and a half at the three-and-a-half-mile mark. Just after passing that flag Harding fell backward on No. 7's legs, which stopped the latter so that he could not use his slide, and this in turn stopped No. 6 for a number of strokes. At this stage, with sometimes five and sometimes six men rowing in the Harvard boat, and with only about a third of a mile to go, the Yale coxswain made known to his apparently completely exhausted crew the disaster which the Harvard crew had met with. He succeeded in putting new life into them, urging them on vigorously to overhaul the floundering Harvard boat and seize this unexpected chance of victory. As a result the Harvard six struggled across the line five or six boat lengths behind the Yale eight. Yale's time was 21 minutes and 12 seconds.

It seems clear that Harding's collapse was the result of a heat prostration pure and simple. He apparently was not exhausted so much as actually taken sick with symptoms of sunstroke and it is probable that the long wait in the hot sun before the race began, contributed materially to his breakdown.

The captain of the Yale '99 and '00 crews was Frederick W. Allen, of Walpole, Massachusetts. The fact that he and Higginson were captains of their respective College crews during these two years, instead of being a cause for some degree of antagonism and suspicion as would have been more or less a matter of course before 1897, now served in some sort as a bond of sympathy and friendship, which developed later into a business alliance and their subsequent joint partnership in the firm of Lee, Higginson & Company.

The four-oared race for the University substitutes, or the second University crews, was rowed about noon on June 28th — the day of the University race — over the first two miles of the four-mile course. The water was very rough and the race consisted practically of a struggle against the elements. Yale was completely outclassed. Harvard led all the way, defeating the Yale crew by six or eight boat lengths.

The Freshman race between the Harvard and Yale crews of '03 was rowed immediately after the four-oared race. Conditions were not good and the time made was slow. Harvard had an easy victory, defeating the Yale Freshman crew by nearly six boat lengths in the two miles.

Harvard 1900 Crew

N. BIDDLE, '00	(160)	HUGH BANCROFT, L. S.	(175)
Bow		C. M. SHEAFE, Jr., L. S.	(167)
H. BULLARD, '02	(162)	C. L. HARDING, '00	(161)
C. B. WOOD, L. S.	(176)	Stroke	
W. SHUEBRUCK, '02	(176)	H. A. WADLEIGH, '00	(103)
W. E. LADD, '02	(176)	Coxswain	

Average weight 170 lbs.

[141]

Yale 1900 Crew

W. B. Williams, '00	(157)	F. W. Allen, '00	(181)
Bow		A. S. Blagden, '01	(172)
H. P. Wickes, '00	(168)	A. Cameron, Jr., '01	(165)
J. H. Niedeken, '00	(170)	Stroke	
P. H. Kunzig, L. S.	(175)	G. P. Chittendon, '01	(111)
J. P. Brock, '00	(183)	Coxswain	

Average weight 171 lbs.

Harvard 1900 Four-Oared Crew

H. P. Henderson, '01	(172)	N. W. Tilton, '00	(175)
Bow		Stroke	
Guy Bancroft, '02	(159)	R. H. Howe, Jr., '01	(105)
G. McConnell, '01	(170)	Coxswain	

Average weight 169 lbs.

1901

Yale won by two boat lengths

Charles M. Sheafe, Jr., class of '98, a student in the Harvard Law School, who rowed at No. 7, was elected captain of the University crew immediately after the race. At the beginning of the fall term, Sheafe decided that in the interests of his chosen profession, he must give up rowing, and Harold Bullard, class of 1902, of Dedham, Mass., was elected captain of the University crew.

The fall season opened in gloom. One of Harvard's very best crews had met with defeat the previous June, an unmerited defeat, it is true, but the moral effect was the same and almost as bad as if it had been overwhelmingly outclassed by Yale. Out of the eight men in the 1900 boat, only Captain Bullard and two others were available as candidates for the crew, and Bullard could be called a veteran solely because of the experience of rowing at No. 2 during the last week of their practice after Higginson broke his leg.

There was no University crew squad in the early season, but all the rowing men were in eights at either the Weld or University boat houses, and called themselves members of the Weld or Newell clubs in the effort to combine club rivalry with class rivalry, with a view to stimulating rowing interest. Senior Weld crew raced Senior Newell crew, Junior and Sophomore crews and even Law School crews did likewise. These races were considered to be for the purpose of selecting the true "class crews."

[143]

On April 11th the final race of the winning crews in the previous elimination contests were rowed on the Charles River Basin between Seniors, Juniors, and Sophomores of the Newell club and a Law School Weld crew. The Junior 1902 crew won. Bullard stroked this crew and Goodell rowed No. 7. The University crew squad as such was organized immediately thereafter, and early in May Mr. Edward C. Storrow took charge of them as coach.

The crews of the past two years had been made up chiefly from the class of 1900 and the three old and well-seasoned oarsmen from the Law School. Now other and newer material had to be developed, but the situation was greatly improved when Hugh Bancroft, one of these Law School men, joined the University squad.

Bancroft took the position of stroke oar and the crew immediately began to develop into fairly good rowing form.

The race was rowed down stream on June 27th and proved to be one of the most interesting and closest ever rowed between these rivals — not that the difference at the finish was so much less than in others, but because of the uncertainty throughout as to the result.

Harvard jumped into the lead at the start and held an advantage of perhaps twenty feet for nearly half a mile. In the next mile Yale led by a dozen feet at times and at others Harvard was ahead. From the two-mile flag to the three, Yale led practically all the way by a few feet and then Harvard passed her and it was thought would now win the race. Near the three-and-a-half-mile flag, however, Harvard faltered and began to slow up. The shell rolled ominously from one side to the other as the coxswain threw the rudder on to avoid striking a flag-staff marking the last half

HUGH BANCROFT, '98, ON THE RIGHT, WITH HIS BROTHER GUY
WHO ROWED ON THE 1902 UNIVERSITY CREW
Sons of William A. Bancroft, '78
In 1901

mile. Yale continued on in her stride although she, too, was clearly much exhausted and won the race by two boat lengths, or eight seconds. Yale's time was 23 minutes 37 seconds.

This crew was peculiarly a one-man crew. Hugh Bancroft '98, at this time in the Law School, rowed at stroke, and was by all odds the most powerful and effective man in the boat. He had been rowing for six or seven years in all, two of them on University crews of 1899 and 1900. It is safe to say that without him the crew would have been decidedly inferior to Yale, while with him at stroke and when the other men were fresh enough to back him up strongly, the Yale crew seemed to have met its match. Towards the end of the race it looked as if the rest of the crew gradually threw more of the burden on him than any one man could carry, while his unusual height was an additional disadvantage to him at stroke with several much shorter men behind him. This experience recalled the story of seventeen years before in the '84 race and Robert P. Perkins '84, who was the Harvard stroke of that year.

Hugh Bancroft, and his brother Guy '02, who rowed in the 1902 University crew, were sons of William A. Bancroft '78, the "Foxey" Bancroft famous as a great oarsman and stroke and as coach of crews in the early '80's. The rowing record of this family has become an important part of college history.

This crew apparently never learned to handle their shell so as to keep it on its keel, it was a proverbially hard boat to row, and the result was that in the race its rolling bothered the men a good deal.

It may be noted here that the loss in weight which had previously characterized all Harvard crews during their stay at New

London now no longer took place. Instead, future crews frequently gained in weight. Nearly every one of the crews throughout the '80's and '90's would lose anywhere from eight to fourteen pounds per man during the two or three weeks' interval between their arrival at New London and the day of the race. Since the crews have been constantly under the eye of a physician, not only has this losing of weight stopped, but almost as it seemed a matter of course, the contrary became the case,—crews would frequently gain two or three pounds on the average. It is not improbable that part of this change is due to the fact that members of later crews were not restricted in the amount of water they were allowed to drink, as was the case with the earlier ones.

Mr. Edward C. Storrow's connection with Harvard rowing as an active coach ended with this season. The Yale crew this year was under the charge of John Kennedy, a former professional oarsman. He continued to serve Yale for several years with almost uniform success.

The four-oared race between the Harvard and Yale second crews was rowed over the two-mile course on the same day as the University race and easily won by Harvard by seven or eight boat lengths.

This year Yale won the class of '04 Freshman race also on the same day, defeating the Harvard Freshmen by ten seconds in the two miles.

In this series of sketches covering twenty years, it is interesting to inquire what if any difference existed between the earliest and the latest Harvard crews of the period in question. The real fact is that in the style of stroke aimed at, the 1882 crew, for instance, differed in no essential respect from the crew of 1901. The difference in the appearance of the two crews, which would have perhaps struck an observer as rather marked, resulted from the difference in the method of instructing or teaching, and the lengthening out of the slides.

The earlier crew was carefully drilled in each single detail of the stroke, throughout the winter on the rowing machines, and in a heavy barge for a month or more after getting on the water, while the later crew was made up of men who had been rowing a full stroke, more or less oblivious of its details, using a light shell and doing considerable racing.

As a result the earlier crew was stiffer than the later and considerably more precise in its movements. The real danger with the earlier method of teaching was that the stroke might be unbalanced, and that the one great essential to speed, namely, a hard push off the stretcher from catch to finish, might be lost sight of among all these careful studies over the other and less important details. This indeed sometimes happened, notably with the Harvard University 1888 crew and the Columbia University 1896 crew. Such overwhelming defeats as these two crews sustained would be practically impossible in case of a crew which pushed off the stretcher strongly and well together, without overemphasizing the catch, no matter how carelessly the rest of the stroke was executed.

Until professional coaches learned that the heavy eight-oared shells were able to keep so much greater headway than the singles and fours to which they had been themselves accustomed, they were too much inclined to disregard the recover, as indeed could be done to a large extent with the lighter boats, and they let their crews rush to the full reach and so stop the heavy eights, but as time went on they gradually discovered that eight-oared crews must learn perfect control of the recover, as being hardly less essential a contribution to speed than the drive from the stretcher itself. This inaptitude on the part of most professionals had some effect on all college crews for many intervening years.

In the case of these two crews twenty years apart in date, to say that they rowed different "strokes" as expressed in the newspapers, is grossly misleading, or to say that the later crew was faster than the former was a fact not susceptible of proof, but clearly the later crew looked as though it did its work more easily and with greater freedom of motion than the earlier one. Furthermore it had the advantage of more carefully studied rigging, which in the case of the earlier crew admitted of their sliding but twelve or thirteen inches to a point five inches back from a line drawn at right angles across the boat from the pin.

Harvard 1901 Crew

R. H. Goodell, '02	(165)	H. Bullard, '02	(167)
Bow		J. Lawrence, Jr., '01	(175)
D. D. S. McGrew, '03	(171)	Hugh Bancroft, L. S.	(179)
R. F. Blake, Gr. Stu.	(161)	Stroke	
W. Shuebruck, '02	(179)	E. W. C. Jackson, '02	(107)
J. B. Ayer, Jr., '03	(175)	Coxswain	

Average weight 170 lbs.

Yale 1901 Crew

C. B. WATERMAN, '01	(164)	P. H. KUNZIG, L. S.	(175)
Bow		A. S. BLAGDEN, '01	(172)
H. S. HOOKER, '02	(170)	A. CAMERON, Jr., '01	(165)
T. R. JOHNSON, M. S.	(178)	Stroke	
R. BOGUE, '03	(165)	G. P. CHITTENDEN, '01	(111)
P. L. MITCHELL, '01	(170)	Coxswain	

Average weight 169½ lbs.

Harvard 1901 Four-Oared Crew

M. H. BROWNELL, '02	(150)	W. JAMES, Jr., '03	(162)
Bow		Stroke	
R. S. FRANCIS, '02	(170)	R. H. HOWE, Jr., '01	(110)
R. DERBY, '03	(167)	Coxswain	

In General

A natural inquiry is, why did Harvard for thirteen years between the victories of 1885 and 1899 succeed in turning out but a single winning crew?

In a general way the answer is that the College had no one competent rowing teacher to see that men were properly instructed, a teacher who was either constantly on hand himself or saw to it that proper assistant teachers were there in his absence. By this is meant teachers not alone for the University crew candidates, but also and especially for Freshman and class crew candidates.

No man nowadays who had never played tennis, or golf, or skated, or ridden a horse, would expect to learn to do any of these things, even in the most rudimentary way, without taking lessons from some professional teacher who knew the game, and was reputed to know how to teach it.

The rowing novice at Harvard, however, was turned loose with seven others as ignorant as himself, and after some form of drill under a teacher who perhaps was personally unskilled, and was almost certainly unaccustomed to teaching, he was expected to row a class race or other short-distance contest. If he happened to take to it naturally and was sufficiently robust, he might eventually find himself in the University crew.

If, however, on his own initiative when first coming to College he had taken up single sculling and obtained a little help and advice from some of the professional scullers to be found on the river in his day, he might have learned in that way more rowing in two or three weeks than in as many years spent in pulling at an oar in one of the organized eights.

The various coaches we had for the University crews were perfectly competent to shake together men who had acquired watermanship and a mastery of the important fundamentals of the stroke, so that they might have turned out fast and able eights to represent the College against Yale crews, but as a matter of fact a coach seldom had even one such man on his entire squad. The best they could do was to try in the short time allotted to them to correct the faults of form acquired in ignorance and neglect and trust to luck as to the watermanship.

During a large part of this period the College authorities discouraged the employment of professional oarsmen as rowing teachers, and indeed it is quite probable that at this particular stage in the history of American eight-oared rowing there were extremely few professionals competent to undertake the work.

It seems, however, as if the employment of almost any one would have been an improvement on the conditions as they actually existed. The Weld boat club did engage a man for a few years, with the result that in his time the rowing there was distinctly better than at the University boat house.

We must recognize the fact that had the elementary teaching been ever so thorough, Harvard would still have been at some disadvantage because Yale's rowing during the entire period was under the management and control of so able and experienced a director as Robert J. Cook.

For some reason the records of the times made by crews have always been a matter of great interest to rowing men and to the public. At New London a crew will win its race over the four-mile course in about twenty-five minutes against a head wind and the next year with no wind the winning time may be twenty-one minutes, and a third year close to twenty minutes.

The fact is that the force of the tide varies greatly on the same course, and even on different parts of the course, and none of these records are of the slightest value as a basis for comparison of the speed of crews of different years.

Cornell crews on a lake are able to establish comparative records which may be very useful, and her records made when no wind is blowing are extremely interesting and, moreover, helpful to the coaches.

At New London, however, it might not happen once in a hundred years that any two four-mile races took place under identical conditions of tide and without any wind throughout the four miles, and even if they did no one would be likely to be aware of the fact. The water there is a mixture of fresh and salt, and after a heavy rainstorm there will frequently be a surface current running out even when the tide is actually rising. At such times, when the tide turns and is at half ebb, the fastest records have generally been made by the crews rowing down stream.

As a matter of argument and discussion it may be profitable to debate the official records and claim that this or that crew had more or less help from the tide on one day than on another, but as affording even an approximate basis for estimating the comparative speed of crews at New London, their time records in the races are wholly useless.

It was not unusual for the public in forecasting the result of a race to assume that the heavier of the two crews would surely win, especially if the difference in weight was at all pronounced.

There can be no greater absurdity than this. There is no more reason for stating that a good four-mile crew should weigh, say, one hundred and seventy-five pounds per man than there would be for making the same claim for a successful baseball nine.

A man below the average size cannot handle the heavy oar and does not possess the necessary reach. He is usually lacking in the chest dimensions needed to allow of the heart expansion incident to hard and long rows, and his wind probably will not be good enough. Any other man, however, who is adaptable, quick in his movements, and can row, may or may not be especially heavy, and yet be a very useful oarsman. Of two crews each made up of eight men of absolutely equal skill and agility, the one with the greater strength, not weight, should win.

In selecting and training crews previous to 1900 the men had to be picked out almost a year ahead and then taught to row; consequently it was thought wise to choose first the best physical specimens and later weed out those that did not prove to be adaptable. It often happened, however, that some big powerful men remained in every crew, who were really very ineffective oarsmen.

In the 1882 crew the two most effective and powerful men were probably Charles P. Curtis, stroke, whose winter weight was 159 pounds, and Robert P. Perkins, No. 3, who weighed 195 pounds early in the season. Curtis was the lightest man in the crew, but the effectiveness of these men came from their strength and skill and had nothing whatever to do with their weight. James J. Storrow weighed 153 pounds in the 1885 race, but was the most effective oar in the boat, although next to the lightest.

On the other hand it is useless to argue, as some do, that a crew of good oarsmen made up of men weighing 150 pounds each, will row faster for a mile, say, than another crew of 170-pound men.

It all depends on the skill of the men and not on their weight. If the 170 pounders are active enough to hold a stroke at thirty-eight to the minute and row as well as the lighter crew, they should perfectly well win such a race.

Doubtless a tall man, well proportioned, can row a long stroke of given measurement with less effort than a short man, and the tall man may be very much above the average weight, but with him the weight is a mere incident and in itself gives him no advantage over the short man, his size merely making it easier for him in the first instance to learn to row.

A really good fast four-mile crew would also be a fast and winning crew for any intermediate distance.

Yale's very fast four-mile crew of 1888 averaged about 164 pounds and their slow crew of 1891 averaged nearly twenty pounds more. A man should certainly be big enough to stand the work, and, if unusually large, he must be active enough to be able to so handle himself as to push his fair share of the boat.

Fred W. Smith '79, who rowed at No. 7 in the '78 and '79 crews, combined such extraordinary skill and activity with unusual strength and size that he was actually provided with an oar with a larger blade than the other men on his crews. It was not his great weight, nearly 200 pounds, which indeed was incidental, but the combination of the other qualities he possessed, which made him remarkable and which have probably not been surpassed since his time.